Inside the Higher Education Space
Governance, Quality Culture and Future Directions – A Malawi Perspective

Ignasio Malizani Jimu

Langaa Research & Publishing CIG
Mankon, Bamenda

Publisher:
Langaa RPCIG
Langaa Research & Publishing Common Initiative Group
P.O. Box 902 Mankon
Bamenda
North West Region
Cameroon
Langaagrp@gmail.com
www.langaa-rpcig.net

Distributed in and outside N. America by African Books Collective
orders@africanbookscollective.com
www.africanbookscollective.com

ISBN-10: *9956-552-08-9*

ISBN-13: *978-9956-552-08-5*

© Ignasio Malizani Jimu 2022

All rights reserved.
No part of this book may be reproduced or transmitted in any form or by any means, mechanical or electronic, including photocopying and recording, or be stored in any information storage or retrieval system, without written permission from the publisher

About the Author

Ignasio Malizani Jimu received university education in Malawi, Botswana and Switzerland. He works for the Malawi University of Science and Technology (MUST) as head of indigenous knowledge systems and practices department. His previous engagements include Associate Professor of Geography at Mzuzu University (2009 – 2014), Quality Assurance Manager (2014 – 2017) and Chief Executive Officer for National Council for Higher Education (2017-2021). His scholarly contributions have appeared as book chapters and articles in: The African Developmental State? Lessons from Botswana and Uganda (CODESRIA, 2005), Forces for Change: Informal organizations in Africa (War on Want, 2006), Transboundary Water Governance in Southern Africa: Examining underexplored dimensions (Namos, BICC and DCAF, 2009), Africa's Informal Workers: Collective agency, alliances and transnational organizing (Zed Books, 2010), Emerging Trends in Assets Recovery (Peter Lang, 2013) and various articles published by the following journals: PULA Botswana Journal of African Studies; Africa Development; Physics and Chemistry of the Earth; Africology: The Journal of Pan African Studies; Journal of African Media Studies; and Modern Africa: Politics, History and Society. He is the author of the following books: Urban Appropriation and Transformation (2008), Peri-urban Land Transactions (2012), and Moving in Circles (2016).

Dedication

To my granny Anne Elizabeth Mussa

Acknowledgement

I wish to thank my colleagues and co-workers in the higher education sector who have shared insights, reflections, and lessons covered in this book. Some of the chapters were conceived while I was working for the National Council of Higher Education (NCHE). However, the drafting of all the chapters to their current form was realized while working for the Malawi University of Science and Technology (MUST). I wish to thank friends and colleagues associated with these institutions, those I have worked with closely over the years and have to some degree helped to sharpen my understanding of the higher education policy context and complexity, its dynamics, stakeholders and governance. My spouse, children and family at large have been fountains of support in the writing of this book. Per tradition of academic writing, while preparing the manuscript, I relied on published works of others, and the sources that were used have been duly acknowledged. At different times, I was privileged to share some thoughts expressed in this book to various audiences, therefore, it is also right and proper to acknowledge their positive feedback. I wish to thank Professor Francis Nyamnjoh for the mentorship and support spanning two decades and in particular, for the realisation of this book. While I share the strengths of this book, the weaknesses are wholly mine. I am responsible for the content and shortfalls in structure, presentation or argument. Finally, the contents of this book do not represent the views or positions of any of the institutions or persons mentioned above or the publisher.

Table of Contents

Acknowledgements v

Abbreviations viii

Chapter 1: Inside the Higher Education Space 1

**Chapter 2: Purpose and Inclusion in
   Higher Education** 17

**Chapter 3: Stakeholdership and Quality
   of Higher Education** 29

**Chapter 4: Operating Context and Quality
   Culture in the Private Higher Education
   Subsector** 57

**Chapter 5: Peer Review as a Quality
   Control Process** 69

**Chapter 6: Quality Rating of Higher
   Education in Malawi** 79

**Chapter 7: Setting and Operating Quality
   Assurance Units in Higher Education
   Institutions** 93

Chapter 8: The Future of Higher Education 123

References 141

Abbreviations

AAU	Association of African Universities
AEF	Accreditation and Evaluation Framework
AQRM	Africa Quality Rating Mechanism
HAQAA	Harmonization of African Higher Education, Quality assurance and Accreditation
HEI	Higher Education Institutions
INQAAHE	International Network of Quality Assurance Agencies in Higher Education
MANEB	Malawi National Examinations Board
MIE	Malawi Institute of Education
MSCE	Malawi School Certificate of Education
MUST	Malawi University of Science and Technology
NCHE	National Council for Higher Education
NCST	National Commission for Science and Technology
NESIP	National Education Sector Investment Plan
NESP	National Education Sector Plan
NGO	Non-Governmental Organisations
NQF	National Qualifications Framework
ODL	Open Distance Learning
QA	Quality Assurance
QAU	Quality Assurance Units
SAQAN	Southern Africa Quality Assurance Network
SARUA	Southern Africa Regional Universities Association
SDG	Sustainable Development Goals
TEVET	Technical, Entrepreneurial and Vocational Educational and Training

Chapter 1

Inside the Higher Education Space

The scope of the higher education space is expansive. It encompasses a broad array of postsecondary education and training institutions whose core business combine teaching (education and training), generation through research and application of knowledge, innovations, skills and technics; adaptation of technology and innovation transfer, and community service.[1] These aspects represent the totality and mission of higher education. A unique feature of higher education institutions (HEIs) is that they educate and certify (warrant) learning. Hence, the term higher education as used in this book refers to institutions that manifest most of the features stated above, in particular, in terms of what they do as their core business, how they conduct their academic processes, the dynamic character of their stakeholdership and the governance and management arrangements.

The higher education process involves a diverse set of elements (curriculum, teaching and assessment) and actors (students; their teachers known variously as lecturers, professors, scholars; administrators; the state; alumni; the business sector; the general public etc.) that are engaged in complex ways. The implication is that the mission, the operationalization (management and governance) of higher education, let alone the outcomes and its quality, are not easy to define. In the specific case of quality, it lies on the perception of each beholder, but also assumes different meanings in different contexts (Cadena et al 2018). That is, perceptions of quality may differ for students, academics or faculty, policymakers, employers, the general public, local and international development partners, among others. It suffices therefore to state that in higher education, quality is multidimensional and contextual.

---

[1] The scope is broader for some countries than others. It is quite extensive in industrialized countries. Here higher education provision encompasses universities, academies, colleges and institutes of technology, vocational schools, and universities of applied sciences, trade schools, and career-based colleges that award degrees. Included are also seminaries.

From the students' or learners' perspective quality may mean value for money; needs satisfaction; and alignment of learning to national or international benchmarks. The irony is, drawing on Peter Materu the author of Higher Education Quality Assurance in Sub-Saharan Africa, quality often implies a certain relative measure against a common standard; except that for much of tertiary education such a common standard does not exist. Hence, various concepts have evolved to suit different contexts ranging from quality as a measure for excellence to quality as perfection, quality as value for money, quality as customer satisfaction, quality as fitness for purpose, and quality as transformation of the learner (Materu 2007). Fitness for purpose (the extent to which the institution's academic and support structures and embedded processes are aligned with their chosen mission statements and with those of the institution) or fitness of purpose (the extent to which there is conformity with national policy and framework, which include governance, planning, funding and resource allocation; connecting the processes, the products, and the relevance of the product and services.

The importance of higher education is not solely in the knowledge amassed by the learner but also in the skills, competences and capabilities gained, over above the spirit to learn cultivated in the learner. According to the Africa-America Institute (2015) higher education yields the following significant benefits for both young people and society: better employment opportunities and job prospects, improved quality of life, and greater economic growth. The attainment of knowledge, higher level skills and competences reflected above should benefit individuals who have access to higher education, their family, immediate community and society at large. The pursuit of learning at higher education level should lead to significant and transformative effects that transcend personal needs, social, territorial and political limits and jurisdictions.[2] Besides developing exploitable and exportable skills,

---

[2] The subject has been examined thoroughly in several publication, for example the World Bank's *Higher Education: Lessons of Experience* (1994) a joint UNESCO/World Bank initiative which resulted in the publication of *Higher Education in Developing Countries: Perils and Promise* (2000); the 2002 publication of *Constructing Knowledge Societies: New Challenge for Tertiary Education* underscored the fundamental importance of tertiary education in the development of globally engaged national systems, be they social, political, cultural, or economic and also *The Challenge of Establishing World-Class Universities* by Salmi (2009).

higher education should empower by enabling citizens to understand and make sense of the social, economic and political realities they find themselves in. It should also serve as an important training ground for effective leadership and therefore a nursery for transformative governance agenda. Higher education should influence cultural appreciation and perceptions, challenge harmful traditional practices and taboos that hinder development to the extent that it compromise progressive thinking. The abundance of benefits would arise from the fact that the higher education institutions, comprising universities, colleges, institutes and centres of higher learning, are concerned with the pursuit of learning, research and consultancy, and preparation for service (Msiska 2008).

Generally, the extent to which individuals, societies or nations are able to reap the dividends depend to a large extent on the accessibility, inclusiveness and the quality of higher education availed to them; making inclusiveness and enhanced quality provisioning important pursuits in higher education policy, governance and management. In this view, the cardinal concern is training for high-level manpower requirements of the nation and for problem solving. The training offered and the governance process should be consistent with norms and acceptable conventions of higher education practice. Hence, higher education institutions must demonstrate respect for learning by upholding professional norms of integrity and honesty. It is evident that continuous engagement with quality issues is also critical to successful realization of both quality culture and effective governance. Quality culture implies consistence in the manner by which higher education institutions create new knowledge by research, transfer knowledge by teaching, and facilitate the dissemination and application of knowledge by their relationship with society (Cadena et al 2018). These have a significant impact on reputation and the extent to which higher education institutions are or will be known nationally and internationally.

Governance from a higher education perspective

The term governance is broad though it is used here narrowly to refer to the traditions, practices and institutions that determine how authority is exercised (Kaufmann et al 2000). In terms of origins, it can be traced back to 400 B.C but modern usage emphasises justice, ethics, the protection of the wealth and interests of the state and its subjects (Kaufmann and Kraay 2003).

Past and present experiences in higher education in Malawi suggest that form of ownership of higher education institutions can raise complex issues of governance and control. This is true for public higher education institutions established by the state under legislation or decree and have their own separate statutory or corporate identity other than that of a department in the civil service. Apparently, the answer to the question who owns such a public university or college invites the response that the university or college is owned by its governing body despite that the state might claim ownership of assets and exercise discreet control of its operations through appointments to the governing board, financing some or all operations, appointment of senior leadership, and other covert forms of control. Also, the higher education space has been an arena for the contestation of power and authority. The resistance to one party rule and the push for multiparty democracy by the student body in the early 1990s, the academic freedom saga at the then sole public university almost two decades later, and the contestation over equitable selection of students, which appeared to favour or disadvantage some ethno-regional and political constituents. The same can be observed in the private higher education space where proprietorship and leadership forms, and compliance or non-compliance with statutory requirements, suggest the need for governance and management models tailored to the realities of the sector, whether perceived from the structural or functional or business perspectives.

Writing about governance in higher education, Salmi observed that high-ranking universities owe their global standing to three connected factors: concentration of talent, abundant funding and appropriate governance (Salmi, 2009). The importance of the first two factors is uncontested if global rankings of higher education institutions are anything to go by.[3] Globally, universities in every

---

[3] One of the often cited ranking systems is the Times Higher Education ranking which measures an institution's performance in four areas: teaching, research, knowledge transfer and international outlook. international reputation, combining subjective inputs (such as peer reviews and employer recruiting surveys), quantitative data (including the numbers of international students and faculty), and the influence of the faculty (see Salmi 2009) or visit

nation tend to enjoy an enviable concentration of highly learned and talented personnel. Retaining such talent and providing for an environment conducive for the exercise of high level intellectual and thought processes and ground-breaking research are resource intensive endeavours. Eventually, governance has become a key issue relative to the expansion of tertiary education systems globally, diversification of provision as a result of the rise of new institution types, multiplicity of programmes offerings and organisational units within institutions, private provision; new modes of delivery providing for more flexible ways of instruction such as distance learning and e-learning; more heterogeneous student bodies; increased female participation and more mature students enrolled; internationalisation of higher education; and overall recognition of the role that higher education plays in human capital development, research and innovation , which imply that such a sector cannot be devoid of acceptable regulatory norms and practices.

Higher education institutions are expected to adjust rapidly, efficiently and fairly to the expanding and changing demands of society and the labour market. Credible accreditation (a process of review and assessment of quality that result in a decision about whether or not to certify the academic standard of an institution) and quality assurance (a planned and systematic review process of an institution or program to determine whether or not acceptable standards of education, scholarship, and infrastructure are being met, maintained and enhanced) (Materu 2007) processes are needed to ensure that students receive quality higher education and that employers (both public and private, national and international) can have confidence in the quality of education provided to potential employees regardless of the differences in the form of ownership of institutions, where some are public and others private and for profit. The bottom line is better governance features are needed for higher education to remain relevant. There is a need for strong strategic vision, a philosophy of success and excellence and a culture of constant reflection, organisational learning and above all readiness to change and adapt to emerging situations. The pivotal position of governance and management is that increasing access

---

https://www.idp.com/uae/the-university-rankings/ Other ranking systems are Shanghai Ranking and QS Ranking.

and enhancing the quality and market relevance of education are in essence governance issues.

Higher education tier

Higher education institutions differ in terms of size and the level of financial and material investment committed by the proprietors. Besides differences in proprietorship, often size is linked to age, whereby older institutions tend to be well established and some of them exhibit state of the art infrastructure and more often offer a significantly diversified range of disciplines and programmes. There are also remarkable differences in the number of disciplinary fields in which they teach, conduct research and award qualifications. Some new institutions teach and award qualifications in one or two fields only. The differences stated above have implications on the nature of their inputs (students, qualified staff among others), their commitment to core values of higher education, but also the way they organise their production processes, measure output and success; and therefore their overall standing as centres of academic excellence.

In the Malawi context, higher education forms the top tier of the multi-tiered education system comprising basic, secondary and tertiary levels. Basic education includes early childhood development and primary education founded and still retaining a fundamental focus on reading, writing and arithmetic (3Rs); much to the same degree as it were in colonial or pre-independence Christian mission schools. Then, the primary outcome was functional literacy tailored to the mission of Christianizing the heathen native. To date, eight years of formal schooling are for primary education, followed by four years of secondary and two to four years or even more for tertiary and university training and education.[4] The tertiary level, which includes higher education, represents a diverse set of institutions and qualification systems.

The categorization presented above is an oversimplification of a complex reality. The National Education Sector Plan (2008 – 2017) which served as the blueprint for education planning, practice and management for well over ten years depicted in detail the situation

---

[4] The World Bank (2010) *The Education System in Malawi*, World Bank Working Paper No 182.

whereby basic education covers early childhood development (ECD), out-of-school youth, complementary basic education and adult literacy as non-formal education and primary education. Secondary education includes open and distance education and formal education attainable at conventional national, district and community day and open secondary schools, all of which lead to secondary school level qualifications and certification. Teacher training for basic and secondary education are considered separate tiers in the education ladder just as Technical, Entrepreneurial and Vocational Educational and Training (TEVET), which is further subcategorized into formal, village polytechnics and distant learning. Since 2014 the TEVET sector witnessed the birth of community technical colleges and community skills development centres (CSDC), which were later linked to the Skills Development Project (SDP) implemented with financial support from International Development Association (IDA) of the World Bank. The Technical, Entrepreneurial and Vocational and Training Authority (TEVETA) was set up by law to facilitate professional training, harmonization and recognition of TEVET system throughout Malawi. Its primary objective is therefore to ensure a sustainable workforce trained through the TEVET sector and thereby promoting the nation's economic growth through skills development.[5] Articulation of TEVET and higher education qualifications stands out as one of the unresolved issues. For higher education, the subcategories include private, public and open universities (Ministry of Education, Science and Technology 2008).

The analysis of the nature and form of learning taking place within each tier is beyond the scope of this book. Suffice to state that to date major qualifications systems in Malawi are:

a) Primary education, where the major shift to date is the introduction of free primary education (FPE) introduced following the transition to multiparty rule in the mid-1990s,[6]

---

[5] Source: https://www.classbase.com/countries/Malawi/Education-System

[6] One of the earliest analyses of the free primary education was provided by Kadzamira and Ross (2001). In their view, they acknowledged the noble intentions of the initiative to increase access, to eliminate inequalities in participation, and spread awareness of the importance of education. Yet, these aims were affected by disjuncture between policy and practice, such that the quantity of primary schooling was increased at the expense of quality, the expansion of primary schooling increased demand for secondary education,

b) Junior Certificate of Education (JCE) and Malawi School Certificate of Education (MSCE) awarded at half-way and at the end of the four-year cycle of secondary education;[7]
c) Post-secondary certificates of varying durations though the preferred and common options last 1 to 2 years of tertiary education and training;
d) Diplomas of varying durations ranging from 2 to 4 years of tertiary education;
e) Bachelor's degree after 4 – 6 years post MSCE or 2-3 years post diploma;
f) Master's degree after 2 years post bachelor's degree; and
g) Doctor of Philosophy (PhD) following 3 – 5 years of study post master's degree.

Entry to tertiary education is primarily based on the MSCE. The national secondary net enrolment rate (young people aged between 13 and 17 years old) has been very low at 13%, with district level rates ranging from 3% to 23% (Government of Malawi 2012a). A very small percentage of the population proceeds to university or other tertiary institutions as shown in the subsequent section.

---

contrary to policy prescription schooling is still not free given that parents are required to spend money on materials and clothes, as well as the opportunity cost of losing their children's labour input and high dropout rates. In terms of success of the initiative, the 2010/2011 integrated household survey (IHS) showed an increase in the net enrolment rate (NER) in primary schools for children between 6 and 13 years of age from 80% in 2005 to 85% in 2011. It has observed that free primary education propelled a significant jump in enrolments by 1 million pupils, the majority of whom were girls. The effect of the drastic shift was an increase in literacy from 63% to 76%, almost all of it a result of the rise of literacy among women. However, it was noted that half of all pupils dropped out before reaching the fifth class of primary school and before many of them had actually attained functional literacy and numeracy.

[7] Until recently, students could be awarded the Primary School Leaving Certificate (PSLC) after successful completion of the eight years of primary education and Junior Certificate of Education (JCE) following successful completion of the first two years of secondary education. These qualification levels were phased out for reasons related to cost of administering examinations in the case of Junior Certificate Examinations and cost of printing certificates for the Primary School Leaving Certificate. While JCE examinations and certification were reintroduced in 2021, those who pass PSLC examinations do not receive certificates for that level of study.

Access to higher education in Malawi

Access refers to opportunity of people from all backgrounds to enrol into higher education on reasonably equal basis (Usher and Medow, 2010). Broadening access, as a policy goal, would require that deserving learners are accorded opportunity to take advantage of educational opportunities on reasonable terms. It becomes a governance issue if perceived from a perspective that privileges the fostering of the efficiency and sufficiency in the provision of essential goods and services, in this instance, the provision of accessible but also quality higher education. Institutions, structures and processes are expected to operate in a manner that promote openness , transparency and accountability, responsiveness to policy and rule of law, equity and inclusiveness, empowerment, and broad-based participation.

Discussions around access to higher education have been fluid and subject to variable interpretations as access to education beyond primary and secondary school levels is constrained and limited for various reasons, including limited space and capacity to absorb all qualifying students within public higher education institutions and, in the absence of an all-inclusive student loan scheme, the prohibitive fees charged by some private higher education institutions. While merit has been a guiding principle in public university selection, achieving equity at the same time has been an exercise in futility due to underinvestment towards expanding space and under provisioning of teaching and learning materials at higher education level as well as at the other levels. One manifestation in public university admission or selection has been the abhorred district quota implemented until the 1990s and later in the 2000s the equitable access, which combined district allocation, gender, merit and elements of regionalism under what was known as neighbouring district principle. Districts that could not satisfy their quota would cede unfilled or excess space to neighbouring districts within the same region. Regional demographics, perceptions of maladministration of school leaving examinations, entitlement mentality, and politics of maldevelopment featured in the discourse until the policy was abandoned in early 2020.

The higher education sector has gone through tremendous change, one of the main facets being the growth from one to two, then three to four and recently from four to six public universities.

The six public universities straddle a narrow range of programming that includes traditional areas such as education and teacher training, humanities, law, theology, commerce, science, agriculture engineering, nursing, medicine and social sciences. Besides public universities there are private universities which outnumber public universities by almost a ratio of 5:1. Nearly 50 % of the private universities have been established by Christian denominations, reflecting unbroken and continuing presence and influence of the Christian missionaries in the shaping of education systems in Africa.[8] Several of the Christian universities have been established on premises that initially housed pioneer teacher training institutions and some have evolved out of ministerial formation institutes and theological colleges. Initial programming for some entailed upgrading of certificate and diploma programmes in theology and religious studies to degree level, followed by an additional of a few programmes in commerce, public health and nursing and midwifery. Most claim driven by a commitment to serve society and enhance betterment of humanity. The growth trajectory mirrors government's attempt to expand access and to some degree enhance quality and market relevance. Ensuring and assuring quality is a call for greater and concerted commitment to the maintenance of a desired level of performance. In other words, increasing and widening access should not be achieved at the expense of quality and relevance, and achieving that requires commitment from all stakeholders.

The World Bank Working Paper No. 182 (2010) titled Education System in Malawi noted that Malawi has the lowest university enrolment (51 per 100,000 inhabitants) compared to Sub Saharan African (SSA) average of 337 per 100,000. Tertiary enrolment was estimated at 1% of eligible students, the lowest rate in the world (Hall and Mambo 2015). The National Education Policy (2016) echoed the same stating that Malawi had one of the lowest access rates to higher education in the Southern Africa Development Community (SADC) region. Over a five year period from 2015 - 2019, which coincided with the implementation period for a landmark project in tertiary education in Malawi, the Skills

---

[8] The difference is in the purpose. Whereas early missionary schools across Africa were intended to produce literate individuals to take over minor positions in local churches and become functioning church members, in the present the focus is broad.

Development Project (SDP) that was supported by the World Bank and the Government of Malawi, only 21% of the eligible candidates were selected into the then four public universities in 2014/15, 27% in 2015/16, 32% in 2016/17 and 2017/18, and 25% in 2018/19 (Jimu and Sadalaki 2021). Many qualified candidates could not secure space. Therefore, pegged at below 1% (around 0.4 % to ne specific) of the eligible population, Malawi's enrolment stands far below the sub-Saharan Africa average of 5%, the developing countries average of 17% and the world average of 24%.[9] The enrolment rate of 0.4% represents a small improvement of the situation in 2000, when access was barely 0.3% (Ministry of Education, Sports and Culture, Malawi Education Sector- Policy and Investment Framework (PIF). Beyond access are challenges of maintaining quality and relevance as documented in the National Education Sector Plan (NESP) 2008 – 2017 and amplified in the National Education Sector Investment Plan (NESIP) 2020 - 2030. Inadequate and deficient conditions in both public and private higher education institutions do not tally with the general awakening in the population and the appreciation of the place of tertiary education in national development. Promises to make higher education accessible and equitable have not inspired commitments to waive financial contribution, especially for students from disadvantaged backgrounds, with the result that every year growing numbers of students from disadvantaged background are forced to curtail their studies prematurely on financial grounds.

A note on the motivation and methodological approach

At Independence, Malawi inherited an education system that was still in formative stages, and an insignificant and small pool of citizens educated to university level.[10] The postcolonial leadership acted swiftly to establish the first university in 1965 to support the education and training of local talent, ostensibly to fill vacancies in

---

[9] The same trend was noted earlier by the Africa-America Institute (2015) which reported that only 6 per cent of young people in sub-Saharan Africa are enrolled in higher education institutions compared to the global average of 26 per cent. The same report shows that between 2000 and 2010, higher education enrolment more than doubled, increasing from 2.3 million to 5.2 million.

[10] Then the population was less than five million but it has bulged to over 17.5 million by 2018.

the civil service. This was a necessary condition for the gradual realisation of the localisation of the civil service. Nearly six decades later, the needs of an informed citizenry in a democratic dispensation, the imperative to better harness the demographic dividend and to respond innovatively to globalization and the pursuit of sustainable development, require serious reflection first and foremost on the purpose of higher education, its role in national development and hence the need to improve upon indicators of access and equity as well as quality and relevance. Rising demand for increased access has revived interests in the subject of equity, but also the national building project through skills development and equalizing opportunities for poverty amelioration and development. The disturbing reality is the deepening of perceived unequal access to education generally and to secondary and higher education in particular measured against commitments to enhance access as a human right and the pursuit of social justice juxtaposed with the need to push towards realization of sustainable development goals (SDGs). The strong argument regarding inclusiveness is that in the interest of fairness every deserving individual must be given an equal chance to access higher education and its benefits irrespective of income or social characteristics such as gender, disability, place of origin or ethnicity.

Since 2007, when the National Education Sector Plan (NESP) was promulgated, three operative goals have framed the discourse on education in Malawi, namely: increasing access and achieving equity, improving quality and market relevance and enhancing governance and management. These policy areas respond to a triune of disadvantages that have constrained higher education; challenges of low enrolment and perceived underrepresentation of some segments of the population, falling quality and graduate unemployment and lapses in governance and management. Various interventions have been made to operationalize the policy goal of increasing access through a myriad of initiatives, and to achieve equity, for example, gender and district based selection, and harmonisation of selection to public universities, inclusive education initiatives targeting expanding enrolment of female students, those with various disabilities regardless of gender, and also financial support to students from poor and disadvantaged households (Ministry of Education, 2020). The pursuit of quality and excellence has necessitated the creation under statute of various bodies for the advancement of professional practice and quality assurance. The pursuit for quality and relevance has been supported by steps emphasising the need to strike a balance between programme offerings and requirements of the labour market.

This book arises from an intimate association and engagement with key stakeholders in higher education over a period of two decades, including the last seven years at the frontline in the context of setting up a regulatory regime for higher education, developing minimum or threshold standards, designing assessment criteria and tools, conducting assessments for the registration of private higher education providers and accreditation of both public and private providers. Hence, the primary intention is to contribute to a discourse on access and more importantly the enhancement of quality of higher education; the need to consolidate governance and management systems and processes and propagation of quality culture. The discussion is informed by an epistemological perspective anchored in personal experience. It is also anchored in the realization of the need to address various gaps in order to ensure that higher education meets acceptable standards.

Much of the information used in this book was generated qualitatively using methods such as interviews, discussions, participant observation and analysis of notes (Lester, 1999 writing on phenomenological perspective). To the extent that the data derives from everyday conversations, the social order shared is a product of processes of social interaction. Thus, intersubjectivity.[11] is an essential element. Apparently, quite often human beings react to what they perceive as reality in a manner that reflects the meanings assigned to it. As Maria González observed "The nature of what we believe is not only real but also the powerful determinant of all we see. Our relationship to what we know is equally influenced by the assumptions we hold about the nature of reality" (González 2003:77). In practice the epistemological relativism implied supports use of a variety of data collection methods mentioned earlier as well as others such as participant and non-participant observation, conversations, analysis of records, texts, material objects, and reflection and introspection (Vannini 2009).

---

[11] It will be noted that in philosophy, psychology, sociology, and anthropology, intersubjectivity may be understood to mean the relation or intersection between people's cognitive perspectives.

Structure of the book

The book comprises eight chapters, including the introductory chapter. The six core chapters are on the following themes:

i) Purpose and Inclusion in Higher Education
ii) Stakeholdership and Quality of Higher Education
iii) Operating Context and Quality Culture in the Private Higher Education Subsector
iv) Peer Review as a Quality Control Process
v) Quality Rating and Quality of Higher Education in Malawi
vi) Setting up and Operating Quality Assurance Units in Higher Education Institutions

The second chapter reflects broadly on the purpose of higher education. It is argued that a credible and valuable higher education system will be progressive and benchmarked in terms of what is taught as part of the core curricula and the values transmitted about service to society. Such an education should be accessible and inclusive for meaningful impact to be realized. The third chapter takes stock of stakeholder interests in higher education. It highlights the importance of knowing the stakeholders and responding to diverse stakeholder perspectives. It interrogates the dilemma of balancing quality and market relevance on one hand and expanding access, achieving synergies and equity on the other.

The fourth chapter focuses on governance and management issues and practices in private higher education institutions in view of the particular patterns of proprietorship and leadership. Hence, regulation and management processes and practices are examined based on selected case studies. The fifth chapter examines on the basis of other case studies the peer review process as used in higher education regulation. Peer review is often contested by policy makers, users, and those affected by the decisions (especially negative decisions) arising from quality academic reviews conducted using the peer review method. At the heart of the discourse have been concerns about the integrity and professionalism of those called to support quality assurance process as peer reviewers against a backdrop of politicisation of quality assurance decisions.

The sixth chapter looks into the methodological and practical aspects of peer reviewing as a quality control measure in higher education regulation, covering aspects of institutions and programmes. The discussion is based on assessments conducted in the past targeting degree awarding institutions, both public and private. The results showed that in the absence of a robust regulatory system, liberalization of higher education is recipe for low quality provision of higher education. This chapter advocates for a robust regulatory system including well-structured system of self-assessments, peer review mechanisms and continuous monitoring whilst respecting institutional autonomy.

The seventh chapter makes a case for the institutionalization of internal quality assurance units (IQAU) within higher education institutions. Establishment of the units is necessary as a means for championing the cause of quality teaching, research, and service to students, and the community at large. Most higher education institutions are yet to embrace this innovation and the few that have are yet to precisely define the governance structure and terms of reference, and to effectively provide an operational environment conducive to the realization of the objectives for setting up such units. A crucial step in this discourse is the need to move from formalization to institutionalization of quality, enactment of appropriate enabling legislation and statutes to resourcing quality units to the required levels consistent with the need and expectation.

The final chapter responds to this set of questions: how to increase access and achieve equity, how to improve quality and enhance market relevance, and finally how to fix the management and credibility issues, including those related to awards-qualifications and promotions. It responds to a triune of disadvantages; challenges of low enrolment and perceived underrepresentation of some populations, perceived quality lapses in management systems. Hence, it suggests that what matters, over and above enrolment in higher education, is the quality and governance of higher education institutions. It pulls together some contentious issues, including the threat posed by bogus qualifications and misuse of honorary titles, invisibility due to limited impact on society, inadequate or lack of elaborate and symbiotic collaboration with industry.

Chapter 2

Purpose and Inclusion in Higher Education

Introduction

Basic, secondary and tertiary education levels represent phases of progressive learning and therefore denote the depth of learning and training attainable per cycle. Each level is in essence a preparation for progressive learning availed in the next level. Per practice, higher education builds on secondary education; it requires inputs from secondary education just as secondary education depends on the basic level. A purposive higher education would be, among other considerations, aligned to ease the progression and advancement of students exiting secondary education. It will not be pegged at a level that will require bridging arrangements to facilitate entry and success other than for affirmative action and inclusiveness. This chapter will focus on the purpose of higher education and the need for inclusiveness.

In a broad and liberal sense, tertiary education covers all forms of post-secondary education and within this category are teacher, technical, vocational and entrepreneurial education and training and higher education. Assié-Lumumba (2006) suggested that the term higher education embodies all forms of organised learning and training, including all manner of learning experiences and qualifications. Others have delineated higher education to post-secondary education institutions where degrees, diplomas, or certificates are awarded at the end of study (Ayewole 2010). In terms of scope, higher education includes institutions other than universities.[12] This is the understanding envisaged for Malawi and provided for in the National Education Sector Plan and in particular the National Council for Higher Education Act, where higher education means "all learning programmes leading to qualifications registered under the National Qualifications Framework (NQF) but may not include vocational training by a

---

[12] Others are s teacher training institutions, institutes and colleges focusing on medicine, agriculture (and other fields), post-secondary distance education centres, research centres and institutes

vocational training centre under the Technical, Entrepreneurial and Vocational Educational Act."

What distinguishes higher education from other forms of tertiary education and training is that students and thereafter graduates are expected to acquire knowledge, skills and competences appropriate for the level of education and training, ability to contribute effectively to producing knowledge as well as developing critical faculties to a level where they can contribute positively to socio-economic and cultural transformation (Garwe 2015; Nyangau 2014; Thiaw 2007). Higher education does not just include college and university teaching and learning by which students progress to attain higher educational qualifications but also impart in-depth knowledge and understanding, taking students to new frontiers of knowledge (Mishra, 2006). In essence, it implies knowing more and more about less and less, and within that regime of knowledge, developing abilities to ask fundamental questions and seek the truth besides mastery of competences consistent with the field of study.

While recognizing existence of a broad array of topical issues, this chapter will focus on the purpose of higher education. In other words, what should be the purpose of higher education? How to deliver higher education that is empowering and more enabling and therefore transformative? In terms of purpose the clarity sought from the questions posed above is not one of either 'form' or 'substance' but both. The pursuit of quality and excellence is also integral to the discourse.

Purpose of higher education

The value of education is never one of scope (breadth) or intensity (depth) of learning only. Rather, it is one of responsiveness to societal needs and aspirations. Focusing on quality as a measure of value and relevance as it relates to the utility of education, Paul Freire, the author of "The Pedagogy of the Oppressed" is one of the outstanding figures. In "The Purpose of Education", he posed fundamental questions such as: "Why educate? What for?" Freire observed that in his native language, the question "why", or "what are things for", or just "what for", imply "how" and "with whom"

Therefore, the answer to the question why educate depends on the dream, vision, political and ideological position.[13]

The implications on curriculum should arguably be of major concern for higher education authorities in Malawi, Africa, the developing world and perhaps the world at large. It is a question of how to produce a graduate whose knowledge is not just theoretical but also practical, who is problem-solving oriented, and more broadly adaptable and responsive to the needs of industry and society. From the functionalists view of education and society, higher education will have a positive impact only if it is structured to meet the needs of society, transmitting essential values and specialized skills for an economy in transition and in need of a specialized division of labour.[14] Emile Durkheim's view was that educational systems reflect underlying changes in society because the systems are a construct built by society as a means of promulgating collectively held values, beliefs and norms. From this functionalist perspective education is a means for transmitting shared values of society and simultaneously inculcating the specialized skills. At national level, higher education should offer a critical route to economic development through the training of professional personnel such as teachers, doctors, nurses, scientists, engineers, linguists, economists, social workers, and technicians; and the development, adaptation and diffusion of innovations and promoting international competitiveness given that export led growth is associated more with higher than basic or secondary education. Beyond meeting and contributing to material needs are the societal level needs such as promotion of mutual understanding, peace and solidarity, unity and togetherness and consensus which are more likely to be achieved through the promotion of learning of the arts, humanities and social sciences. Education in the arts, humanities and social sciences is therefore vital as it contributes to the preservation and advancement of accomplishments of the past, providing insight into and understanding of the present world and, bequeath tools to create or recreate a better future. It is true that

---

[13] Paul Freire 'The Purpose of Education", Extract from "The 40th Anniversary of the UNESCO Institute for Education", UIE Reports No. 6, 1992. http://www.unesco.org/education/pdf/FREIRE.PDF

[14] Drawn from online resource titled: 'Durkheim's Perspective on Education' https://revisesociology.com/2017/08/22/functionalist-durkheim-role-education/

through the humanities students and society are ably empowered to make moral, spiritual, and intellectual sense of the world. The value of the arts in decision-making, especially on complex ethical issues that confront society is immense. For the curriculum developers, the challenge becomes how to concretize and compartmentalize knowledge, skills and attitudes in the curricula.

To this extent, an elaborate higher education worth the name should be structured and therefore systematic that those exposed to it (youths, adults, men and women alike), would acquire useful knowledge, skills, experience, and progressive attitudes. The expectation should be an education designed and therefore tailored for transformation of the whole person, the individual and society. The products of such an education system would be refined, cultured and above all educated in the true sense of the word.[15] That is, higher education in the broadest sense of the term should engender transformation of the human person in his/her pursuit of wholeness as a social being. This is a call for what John Parankimalil, a Selesian missionary, referred to as the harmonious development of the physical, mental, moral (spiritual), and social faculties, which are in essence critical dimensions of life, for a life of dedicated service to society. A good education system and a good curriculum will embody a broad array of outcomes.[16]

Therefore, in terms of purpose, higher education should directly attempt to respond to social needs, to foster development and propagation of desirable skills, attitudes, motives, beliefs, ethical

---

[15] John Parankimalil (2012) "Meaning, nature and aims of education", https://johnparankimalil.wordpress.com/2012/03/26/meaning-nature-and-aims-of-education/

[16] Nine decades ago, in a chapter titled "Individual Psychology and Education" (1934) John Dewey once noted that: "The purpose of education has always been to everyone, in essence, the same—to give the young the things they need in order to develop in an orderly, sequential way into members of society. This was the purpose of the education given to a little aboriginal in the Australian bush before the coming of the white man. It was the purpose of the education of youth in the golden age of Athens. It is the purpose of education today, whether this education goes on in a one-room school in the mountains of Tennessee or in the most advanced, progressive school in a radical community. But to develop into a member of society in the Australian bush had nothing in common with developing into a member of society in ancient Greece, and still less with what is needed today. Any education is, in its forms and methods, an outgrowth of the needs of the society in which it exists." John Dewey, "Individual Psychology and Education," *The Philosopher*, 12, 1934

reasoning and behaviour. These values are needed more to counter retrogressive tendencies such as individualism, exploitation of the vulnerable and minorities, corruption in public and private institutions, violence, sexual harassment and transactional sex, including what is known in higher education as sex for grades or sexually transmitted grades (STGs)]. Reflecting on the same concern Martin Luther King Jr., in a speech made at Morehouse College in 1948 said:

> "The function of education is to teach one to think intensively and to think critically. But education which stops with efficiency may prove the greatest menace to society. The most dangerous criminal may be the man gifted with reason but no morals. ... We must remember that intelligence is not enough. Intelligence plus character—that is the goal of true education."[17]

It follows that an effective higher education should contribute to the formulation of standards of character, in creating habits of responsibility in conformity with the standards, and consolidation of a culture conducive to the nurturing of individual character and national consciousness.[18] Pertinent questions at this juncture include: has the higher education system served us well? In which specific areas? Where are we lagging behind? How do we progress from here? To respond adequately to the need for character as an ingredient of an education will require radical transformation, a struggle against various forms of resistances to achieve but also entrench a new social order as has been the case since antiquity, from the time of Socrates.[19] A point to be emphasized is that higher

---

[17] 'The Purpose of Education', published in
https://kinginstitute.stanford.edu/king-papers/documents/purpose-education

[18] As Aristotle is reported saying that "Educating the mind without education the heart is no education at all"

[19] Ariel Dillon using Socrates' cave analogy shows how character formation is a challenging issue. Socrates used an analogy of a cave in which humans are chained from birth facing a wall. Behind them, puppet-masters use figurines which cast shadows on the wall in front of the prisoners. Because the prisoners know nothing else, they assume the shadows to be the extent of reality, but what they see and hear is in essence and actually only a small segment of the intelligible world. According to Dillon, the image of the cave evokes Socrates' discourse and representation of false tales and noble lies. Education and higher education in particular, should free individuals and societies from false opinions and

education should be structured and rigorous enough to liberate the learner from the cultural, economic, political, religious and other forms of lies and falsehoods. The pursuit of truth should inspire the quest for transformation of character. Lack of befitting character is a challenge that higher education should aspire to engage with. To realize such an education requires liberating the learning as Paul Freire also put it:

> "Why educate? What for? One of the reasons is precisely to develop the ability to ask good questions, and to refute false answers. There is no real humanistic education, no education for liberation - which means more than education for freedom - if the right to raise questions is denied and if false answers are not refused." [20]

Once again, the education tier best suited to inquiry into such fundamental questions and the advancement and liberation of society is higher education. Realizing that the education system we embraced is not originally ours in terms of origin and its philosophy, rather, it is one among many things imposed by the

---

convictions, as opposed to chaining them. Back to the prisoner analogy, Dillon states that philosophical education is often resisted though it is enlightenment and progressive. So, he asks about what would happen if one prisoner was to be unchained and allowed to leave the cave and become exposed to reality? Dillon is categorical on what would happen: " At first, he would be pained and disoriented by the foreign sights. When told that his experience in the cave was not entirely real, he would rebel- and not without reason. If he tried to look at his new surroundings and the sun directly after leaving the dark cave, he would be blinded and would want to return to the comfort of his familiar past surroundings. Socrates asserts that if someone were to drag him "away from there by force along the rough, steep, upward way, and didn't let him go before he had dragged him out into the light of the sun" the prisoner would fight and be resentful, and even then, would not be able to see everything at once. Instead, his eyes would adjust slowly. First he would see shadows, then reflections in water, then things themselves, then the night's sky, and finally, the sun--which is an image of the good and what is. But once he focuses on what is, he will be happier than ever before and will never want to return to the cave. Furthermore, if he did try to return to the cave and help the other prisoners, they would hate him, calling him corrupt and delusional because their reality is still limited to the shadows in the cave" Ariel Dillon (n.d.) 'Education in Plato's Republic'
https://www.scu.edu/character/resources/education-in-platos-republic/ (accessed on 10th July, 2018)

[20] Paul Freire 'The Purpose of Education", Extract from "The 40th Anniversary of the UNESCO Institute for Education", UIE Reports No. 6, 1992. http://www.unesco.org/education/pdf/FREIRE.PDF

former colonial masters after indigenous institutions, ways of knowing and knowledge transfer were destroyed during colonialism. There is a need to seriously reflect on the necessity of perpetuating this reality, in particular, the indoctrination whose facets and tools include the education system itself, religion, linguistic and cultural imperialism.

Writing on the changing purpose of higher education, Chan (2016) observed that historically, institutions of higher education existed to educate students for lives of public service, to advance knowledge through research, and to develop leaders for various areas of public service. In recent times, higher education institutions are required to prepare graduates to meet not just the current but also the future needs of society and to participate fully in the shrinking global economy. These expectations call for profound changes in the structure and configuration of higher education. The change includes shifts in perceptions of education from solely a public good, appreciation of the importance of private benefit, shifts in focus from national to regional and global perspectives, emergence of colleges and universities structured and modelled on corporate industry with predominantly pro-profit goals and market-oriented values. These changes explain the rise of an industrial model of education thanks to the privatization, commercialization, and corporatization that have already started to alter higher education's traditional mission, and have also begun to inform and encourage increased differentiation in higher education systems. The needs of the labour market, the urge to contribute to problem solving through research, efficiency and accountability for use of resources, both public and private, and inclusivity are important dimensions of this emerging higher education narrative.[21] Thus, it is possible to perceive higher education in multiple ways:

a) Higher education as the production of qualified human resources. In this specific sense higher education is a process in which the learners are counted as products to be absorbed in the labour market and this is a business and industry focused approach to higher education.

---

[21] See Mishra (2006) Quality Assurance in Higher Education: An Introduction.
http://naac.gov.in/images/docs/Resources/Toolkit4Tr_Edctn_Institution/QAHE-Book.pdf

b) Higher education as training for a research career where the focus can be on preparing scientists and researchers who would continuously develop and expand the frontiers of knowledge. Emphasis may also be on enhancing the ability to produce publications and transmission and translation of the academic rigour into quality research.
c) Higher education as the efficient management of teaching provision. To date teaching is the core function of educational institutions and higher education institutions are expected to be efficient in the management of teaching-learning provisions. An important indicator of teaching efficiency is higher completion rate and quality of graduates.
d) Higher education as an enterprise of extending life chances. To this extent higher education should provide an expanded range of opportunities to participate in the development process by individuals and communities through flexible and continuing education mode.

While embracing the multiple dimensions stated above, the vision and mission of higher education in Malawi is still focused on the production of human resource. The key aspect is the expectation that higher education should and ought to be responsive to national needs and priorities. Values of community involvement and participation should be infused in the system until it becomes a norm for graduates and alumni to know that no solution to a problem should ever be imposed on a people in a top-down manner without genuine participation of those to be impacted. This is also a call for better positioning of higher education institutions and proper alignment of programmes to industry and societal needs. A progressive higher education system should also provide an environment suitable for developing and nurturing of entrepreneurs, but also an open, competitive and progressive thinking. The curricula should empower the student to challenge injustices be they economic, social or political. The overall experience in the classroom and outside it should contribute to the formation of responsible citizens and not subjects. Liberation from all forms of backwardness and oppression and pursuit of radical transformation from subjects to citizens in this sense should become a core motive of higher education. Higher education should also contribute to the shaping of the cultural and political conscience of society where fundamental freedoms will be respected, protected and promoted. A complementary political project of self-reliance should be promoted.

The implications are enormous in terms of what higher education institutions should actually do or strive to be. Higher education institutions should enhance the scope of their programming. For the purpose of industrialization, the future is science, technology, engineering, and mathematics (STEM). The management of higher education provision should ensure achievement of various operative goals in teaching, research and innovation and meaningful engagement with community and industry. It requires progressive shift in the areas of course planning and design, teaching and learning support regimes. Real transformation will come if providers and consumers of higher education can accept and begin to take full responsibility for the quality of higher education; whether higher education is perceived as a service or a commodity and private good. The proposition provided above is pertinent given the privatization and commercialization of higher education[22] taking root in public colleges and universities. Such tendencies include charging of commercial fees for mature entry undergraduate programmes, dollarization of fees for postgraduate programmes and rationalization measures that appear to defy the service function of public higher education. Private providers capitalize on liberalisation to overcharge students tuition and non-tuition fees, for instance, admission, module exemption, supervision and graduation fees. In the absence of bursaries targeting the needy, those who may not afford the high fees self-exclude from pursuing higher education. Fees may rightly be perceived as an exclusionary instrument.

Making higher education inclusive

Besides making higher education accessible through removal of barriers to entry, it is imperative to be inclusive and responsive to learning needs of all. Inclusiveness requires eliminating barriers to participation for all learners other than those related to prohibitive

---

[22] See a letter from a concerned citizen to the editor titled 'Public universities killing tertiary education', *The Daily Times*, January 4, 2019.

admission criteria. Achieving inclusiveness, which is truly rights-based require all aspects of the education system to be reviewed with a view to eradicate pockets of resistance which militate against inclusion of disadvantaged population groups. Malawi like many developing countries is struggling to provide resources for all levels of learning. Economic liberalization policies pursued since the 1980s, massification and cross-border provision have exposed the fragile and precarious situation. At the peak of the first and second waves the Covid 19 pandemic forced closure of all educational institutions for many months, and attempts to transition to virtual learning proved disastrous especially for learners from disadvantaged backgrounds. The technological gap implied that learners from rural and poor families could not participate and equity was sacrificed. As observed by Walton (2018) the pressure to adopt inclusive education comes with scant recognition of ways in which the history of colonialism and underdevelopment compound the problems of exclusion in countries of the Global South. The implication is that in countries that have been struggling to guarantee access to quality basic education except for a selected few, a majority of learners have had to accept deplorable deterioration of education standards. Calls for inclusive education have therefore tended to receive less attention and at worse pushed to the peripheral on the pretext that it is idealistic. Drawing on Ainscow (2014) calls for contextually appropriate understandings of inclusive education have been made and one of the maxims has been the call that it should be contextually determined (see Jimu and Sadalaki 2021). The sad reality is the exclusion of learners with special needs, other than those alluded above. Ncube (2014) writing for Zimbabwe observed that people with special needs have sometimes been excluded from the higher and tertiary education system simply because the system does not have structures and mechanisms in place to respond to the needs of their peculiar situation. Where lack of suitable facilities has been accepted as an excuse for not admitting learners with various disabilities, in the long term, disability remains invisible within higher education space (Kochung 2011). State commitment is therefore required in line with the Convention of the Rights of People with Disabilities (UN 2006) which provides that it is an obligation of state parties to ensure that persons with disabilities have access without discrimination and within the same conditions as the rest to higher education, professional training, adult education and lifelong learning (Moriña 2016). On a positive note, Morina (2016) observed that a significant number of countries have launched actions to make higher education including college and universities more accessible for people with disabilities, hence becoming progressively more committed to the processes of inclusion (Barnes 2007; Jacklin et al. 2007). Pertinent to inclusiveness are fairness and equity, uniform opportunity to access but also participate, cognizant of diversity of learning needs (Blessinger (2018). It follows, as Čerešňová (2018) observed that inclusivity should be an aspect of quality higher education and should embody equity in programming, recruitment of staff, admission of students and delivery of education and training.

Concluding reflections

Higher education should be structured to serve both individual and societal purposes. For instance, higher education should lead to attainment of employable skills that open possibilities for better-paying, more prestigious and rewarding careers. Higher education should be able to place individuals that have access at an advantage in society, including shifting of power relations e.g. gender relations; and enable citizens regardless of their gender or social standing to understand and deal with difficult and divisive issues, to challenge the fundamentalism of ethnicity, tribalism and regionalism, which until to date have made it difficult even for well-educated and very pious to make rational decisions, act piously, and to hold political leaders and public officials truly accountable. The benefits of such an education can be enjoyed only where the education offered is relevant, meeting reasonable standards of quality and is also accessible to a majority and inclusive at the same time. Improving access and providing quality higher education should empower the poor, the weak and the voiceless. The consequences of poor quality higher education are grave. They may include poor policy choices affecting key sectors of education, economy, politics, family life, work and citizenship. Therefore, there is a need for serious reflection on the purpose of education and of higher education in particular. Equally important are concerns of gaps in participation of stakeholders in defining the purpose and shaping the quality agenda of higher education. It is necessary to make higher education and universities centres for the production of knowledge and development of ideas, skills, values and attitudes for engaging with development challenges (see Msiska, 2008). A responsive higher education system cannot be anything but a product of its society, an embodiment of its diverse stakeholder perspectives.

Chapter 3

Stakeholdership and Quality of Higher Education

Introduction

The term 'stakeholder' embraces individuals, groups of individuals and institutions that influence the success or failure of an entity or organization, including higher education institutions, which are the point of focus in the context. This chapter dwells on the subject of higher education stakeholders in the context of Malawi. From identifying and therefore knowing key stakeholders, it analyses the roles, responsibilities, demands and expectations of each stakeholder category. In view of the pillars for education introduced in the previous chapters, the discussion will revolve around the nexus of access, quality and market relevance, and management of higher education. Oftentimes perceptions of quality are varied, sometimes conflicting and generally dependent on the diversity of stakeholder interests, experience and expectations. Indeed, stakeholders have effects on the activities, processes, procedures and outcomes of the higher education institutions as regulators, competitors and sources of opportunities or threats. Hence, this consideration of stakeholders and their roles is important to the extent that it delves into relationships that affect the operationalization of programmes, management and quality assurance regimes and practices. A point to be emphasized is that there are linkages, convergences and divergences in interests of different stakeholders, and it is such linkages, convergences and divergences that are worth exploring and where necessary strengthening in order to build a strong higher education sector with robust quality culture.

The diversity of stakeholders and the linkages among them often mirror the complex nature of the core business of higher education, which includes transmission, propagation, application and synthesis of existing knowledge; the generation of new knowledge to expand frontiers of the known worlds of science, technology and culture through research and application of the knowledge, skills and competences to everyday life. Each facet entails a particular set of users and clientele whose needs, aspirations and visions do not always converge in a neat fashion. Therefore, there is value in knowing, identification and management of diverse stakeholder interests for an effective management regime to evolve, which implies effective decision making, planning, identification of needs and problems and ultimately knowing who may exert influence or shape the direction of quality and management processes within and between institutions and the higher education sector more broadly. Chapleo and Simms (2010) reduced the analysis of stakeholders in higher education to four fundamental questions: Who are the stakeholders? Which stakeholders are of greatest priority to a higher education institution? Which factors affect prioritization of each stakeholder? What are the key issues in managing the stakeholder groups?

For higher education, one may isolate the following stakeholders: students, alumni, management of each institution, parents or guardians, other education institutions including secondary schools, colleges and universities, accrediting bodies and agencies, suppliers of goods and services used by higher education institutions, employers of graduates, taxpayers, non-governmental organisations (NGOs), the government, and academic staff, both individually and collectively in disciplinary groups and as members of the organized labour movement (staff unions and advocacy bodies) (Marshall 2018). It is possible to think of higher education institutions as a partnership of faculty and administrators, students and alumni, trustees, and society at large. The interplay of stakeholder interests will be analysed in relation to the overarching goals for higher education, which as stated earlier are increasing access and equity, quality and market relevance. The major dilemma has been balancing quality and increased access amidst challenges of underfunding, underinvestment in infrastructure and human capital development and poor performance rating for outsourced services which has become a norm in public institutions. Apparently, outsourcing of services was forced on public higher education institutions as a package of reforms heralded as liberalization by the World Bank and International Monetary (IMF).

Focusing on quality, this chapter shows that the primary stakeholders are the students, teachers (lecturers and professors), and management of higher education institutions. Beyond these internal stakeholders are other equally critical actors, namely: the government, professional regulatory bodies, employers, parents, non-teaching staff working for higher education institutions and national regulatory bodies. However, in terms of focus this chapter will dwell on five stakeholder groups selected for their direct and demonstrated roles in respect to promoting the core mandate of higher education. These key stakeholders, presented not in the order of importance are: the state or government often exercising authority and oversight through the Ministry of Education (MOE), which is the policy holder, the National Council for Higher Education (NCHE) as the state regulatory body, higher education institutions as providers of higher education, students and alumni as primary customers and finally the industry as the user of the higher education product. In essence, higher education students are the most important stakeholder group on campuses of higher education institutions, while alumni tend to be ambassadors of their alma mater. The quality of their training and disposition of alumni in industry mirror and represent the character and quality of the graduate expected from those still studying in the higher education institutions. The maxim is that the primary responsibility for ensuring quality education rests with the higher education institutions and fundamentally the locus of primary activity for the promotion, propagation and consolidation of quality assurance efforts. The rest of the stakeholders play secondary or facilitating and enabling roles. This analysis goes beyond identification of the key stakeholders. It encompasses consideration of whether the stakeholders are doing enough, the shortfalls and the need for synergies for effective engagement and management of both access and quality processes. Further, it examines the operational context and the uneasy balance between some stakeholders, including the questions of compliance with the law and policy.

The role of the state in higher education

The role of the state is that of promoting and regulating higher education by providing the legal framework and policy direction. The state is also a key partner providing and sometimes coordinating financing of public higher education. To that effect the state stands out as the policy holder, the giver of the law and provider and protector of the higher education sector and anchoring its integrity. For Malawi, this expectation was articulated explicitly as follows:

> "The Ministry of Education, Science and Technology is the custodian of the Malawi's Education Sector as well as all matters relating to Science and Technology. The Ministry is the Government arm that is responsible for providing policy guidance and direction on all education, science and technology issues."[23]

The Ministry has developed various policy instruments, including the National Education Policy and National Education Sector Investment Plan (NESIP). The Ministry is also the custodian of the Acts of Parliament establishing all public universities, the National Council for Higher Education and the Higher Education Students Loans and Grants Board (HESLGB), among many other entities in the education sector. Within these legal and policy frameworks the Ministry contributes to meeting human resource development needs. Resource and policy limitations notwithstanding, the state has to a significant degree promoted higher education and quality provision financially and by setting up institutions that support critical areas of higher education management.

From the perspective of the state, teaching and learning in higher education have been promoted through investment in infrastructure, training, and budget support towards procurement of teaching and learning materials. Support to lower levels of education and training in early childhood development, basic and secondary education indirectly serve the interests of higher education given that students who enrol for higher education are products of primary and secondary education. It means that the level of investment and commitment to quality at these lower levels have catalytic effect and therefore essential and complementary to the achievement of quality outcomes at higher education level. Towards these ends the state has over time established schools, colleges, institutes, and boards with specialized functions and tailor-made mandates. For instance, the Malawi Institute of Education (MIE) is responsible for curriculum and development of teaching and learning materials for primary and secondary levels, while the

---

[23] Ministry of Education, Science and Technology website:
http://www.malawi.gov.mw/index.php?option=com_content&view=article&id=21&Itemid=21

Malawi National Examinations Board (MANEB) is responsible for standardization of teaching and learning through public examinations based on predefined syllabi. Other bodies with significant influence include the National Commission for Science and Technology (NCST) whose mandate is to promote research and innovation, the Higher Education Students Loans and Grants Board (HESLGB) for the management of loans and grants to deserving and needy students, the National Library Service (NLS) responsible for establishing, equipping, maintenance and development of public libraries and National Council for Higher Education (NCHE) responsible for the regulation of higher education and harmonization of selection of students to public universities.

The state retains the final word on matters of registration of private higher educations. Through the Minister responsible for higher education, the state grants charters, approves registration of institutions, promulgates minimum standards for establishing and operating higher education institutions, define criteria for the accreditation of institutions and above all the accountability for the quality of higher education. Certainly, the legal and policy framework requires strengthening. There is need for a unified higher education act to provide clear and unequivocal legal direction. The challenge with the current set up is that each public university has its own act and that arrangement is not the best possible as it poses serious challenges to coordination and harmonizing relevant practices. The National Educational Policy is biased towards basic and secondary education, hence the need for a higher education policy. Effective implementation of various policy initiatives in the core areas of increasing access and improving equity, quality assurance and market relevance and governance and management have been constrained by resource limitations. Therefore, there is need for better and sustainable funding model for higher education. Over time discussions have tended to focus on increasing government subvention, yet the resource envelope and competing priorities imply that expected improvements have to be achieved without significant increase of funding from government subvention. This is a call for innovative income generation strategies, a business unusual approach to fundraising on one hand and a commitment to efficiency by public higher education institutions on the other. Hence, executive extravagance, abuse and misallocation of funds should be checked.

In order to leverage funding gaps oftentimes the government has sourced foreign financing in the form of loans and grants from bilateral and multilateral financial agencies to build new and modernize existing infrastructure, enhance staff development and support the drive towards quality and market relevance of programmes. In recent times notable interventions have been the skills development project (SDP) and higher education science and technology (HEST) bankrolled by the World Bank and African Development Bank respectively.[24] Major developments under the two projects have been improvements in infrastructure (laboratories, classroom and lecture theatres, satellite centres for delivery of programmes through open and distance learning)[25], support towards development of new demand driven programmes and review of existing programmes with significant input from industry. Perhaps the greatest commitment of foreign investment in the higher education in the last decade was the construction of the Malawi University of Science and Technology (MUST) bankrolled by the government of China. Collectively these projects demonstrate the importance of foreign injection of capital to complement locally generated funds through taxes directed towards public sector investments in higher education. A robust staff development programme in critical areas is a major boost to the capacity of higher education institutions to offer training and research degrees at advanced level much as it is also an important step towards sustainability through continuous training. The capacity to mobilise domestic and foreign finance for higher education broadens the understanding that the state has the primary responsibility of educating the citizen today and in the future even as liberalization and privatization of higher education are gaining ground. It underscores the role of the state towards ensuring that

---

[24] For progress and updates from The Polytechnic, a constituent college of University of Malawi see https://www.poly.ac.mw/news/minister-of-education-inspects-construction-projects-18-09-2017

[25] One of the notable outcomes is the change in perception towards open and distance learning as a mode of delivery. Until 2017, acceptance of ODL was quite low among senior managers in higher education institutions, some of whom were openly skeptical and disdainful, especially of those who do their studies entirely online.

future generations shall have better trained teachers, doctors and nurses, engineers, lawyers, among other significant professions.

The state operates in a context which includes regulatory regimes governing public health and safety standards, employment related laws and taxation which apply to both public and private institutions. The relevance of such laws and standards is appreciated in their impact on the delivery of quality and relevant education and training within the given regulatory framework. The drawback over time has been the inadequacy of state support. The support has been limited to public higher education institutions despite the commitment to broaden access which included milestones arising from the private provision of higher education. The implication has been narrowed space for private higher education institutions which cannot attract bright students from disadvantaged backgrounds for reasons of high tuition fees. The funding challenges for the Higher Education Students Loans and Grants Board is a further constraint as it limits the window of opportunity to access both public and private higher education. Hence, meaningful state intervention as a critical stakeholder calls for adequate funding direct to training institutions and through other institutions established to support access and quality.

Besides setting the agenda through enabling laws and policies and provision of resources, the state should be able to inspire and challenge higher education institutions, both public and private, to pursue academic excellence as an end. Therefore, an important trajectory towards the realization of quality higher education is commitment of state actors to set the tone impressing upon all other stakeholders that mediocrity will not be celebrated. Where academic freedom and institutional autonomy are defining characteristics of the academy, the state has an obligation to provide a framework for the free exercise and protection of the freedom of inquiry, pursuit of knowledge and truth, autonomy required for growth of institutions and the nurturing of unfettered advancement of learning and spirit of inquiry. It follows also that the state has the obligation to challenge those entrusted with the teaching and management functions to think outside the box, beyond matters of access and quality as dictated by the state and endorsed by the international community, to ensure the better governance and accountability of the higher education institution to society. For Malawi, this point was advanced and articulated during the last graduation ceremony of the University of Malawi as a federal institution by its Chancellor who challenged the leadership, faculty, students and the public at large that:

> "Becoming a university is not an automatic process. You can name yourself "a university" without becoming one, if you don't meet what it takes to become a university. The law and statutes will not make you a university automatically. You must earn your status of being a university on the international stage".[26]

It is a reasonable expectation that agencies set by the state to support, promote, regulate higher education would stand for and advance such goals and the pursuit of excellence.

The quality regulatory body

Following the footsteps of many African states that have established bodies responsible for the regulation of higher education known variously as councils, commissions and authorities; the state established a National Council for Higher Education (NCHE) by an Act of Parliament No. 15 of 2011. Bodies performing similar functions in southern and eastern African countries include the national councils for higher education (NCHE) in Namibia and Uganda, councils of higher education (CHE) in South Africa and Lesotho or its variant the Zimbabwe Council for Higher Education (ZIMCHE) in Zimbabwe, the Higher Education Council (HEC) in Rwanda, Commission for University Education (CUE) in Kenya or Commission for Universities in Tanzania (TCU) and the Higher Education Authority (HEA) in Zambia. These bodies operate at national level and in terms of their mandate, they derive authority from national laws with transnational impact enhanced through mutual recognition and membership to quasi regional bodies such Southern Africa Quality Assurance Network (SAQAN) for the SADC or East African Quality Assurance Network (EAQAN) for the East African Economic Community.

---

[26] Extract from the speech of Professor Arthur Peter Mutharika, State President and Chancellor of University of Malawi, 3rd Congregation of University of Malawi held in The Great Hall, Zomba, 8th November, 2019.

In April 2012, the National Council for Higher Education was appointed and its Secretariat was set up two years later in May 2014. The NCHE Act envisage internal and external quality regimes founded on Minimum Standards designed to anchor the establishment and management of higher education institutions. The tasks and responsibilities previously exercised by the government through the Credentials and Evaluation Committee (CEC) were therefore on the passing of the NCHE Act were transferred to NCHE.[27] Hence, matters related to quality development and quality assurance within higher education in Malawi are within the scope, functions and powers of the Council. The Council registers private higher education institutions and accredits both institutions and programmes of public and private higher education institutions. Yet, until recently the role of the NCHE was less understood and appreciated. Cartoonists, comedians and some administrators in higher education institutions would describe NCHE as a toothless dog. Sentiments pointing to the ineffectiveness of NCHE were propagated without due regard to the operating legal context.

Registration and accreditation are informed by best practice in higher education regulation which includes self-assessment and peer review processes which serve the purpose of ensuring the provision of quality education through processes that are transparent and responsive. Self-assessment is a process through which higher education institutions provide information required by the quality assurance body. The self-assessment report is a foundation on which an external review team builds their understanding of the institution or programme. The Council monitors, registered and accredited higher education institutions and implementation of registered and accredited degree programmes. Obligations owed to the Council by registered and accredited higher education institutions include: commitment to a culture of quality, regular self-assessment of quality provision; self-assessments leading to accreditation and the obligation to commit to a process of continuous improvement which require that institutions implement

---

[27] CEC was involved in the accreditation of institutions/programmes for the purpose of training and career advancement in the civil service. It drew its membership from different government departments. Its major shortfall was lack of legal authority, despite enjoying the support of the state.

recommendations arising from external and internal review processes.

In carrying out its responsibilities NCHE applies standards of quality assurance approved by the Minister for education. The standards are national to the extent that they define nationally agreed minimum requirements for operating higher education institutions and the offering of higher education qualifications in Malawi. The standards are also international to the extent that they are benchmarked to best practices in the higher education space in the region. Therefore, the standards ought to provide a reasonable measure of quality and ensure comparability of higher education and training in Malawi to the best within Africa and around the world and effective implementation is necessary as an endeavour to promote and ensure a culture of quality and excellence. Hence, compliance to minimum standards for registering private institutions and programmes; compliance to criteria for accrediting higher education institutions and programmes; continuous monitoring of standards prevailing in higher education institutions and degree programmes; providing information and advice to higher education institutions in matters related to quality assurance and quality enhancement; and promoting international cooperation with like-minded organisations in the region and further afield in the area of quality assurance are important milestones.[28]

A cardinal practice in registration and accreditation of institutions or programmes is transparency and readability of quality review procedures and conformance to set standards and criteria. It is also pertinent that monitoring activities are instituted to support effective consolidation of internal quality management systems and enhanced compliance in areas such as quality of infrastructure (lecture rooms, laboratories and accommodation for staff and students), admission criteria for students and recruitment of lecturers, and also standards of teaching, assessment, research and industrial attachment and award of qualifications. In the interest of inculcating a culture of quality and excellence, support towards continuous development of the internal quality assurance systems is essential. Likewise, it is essential to ensure that the public is well informed of the decisions on or the changing status of institutions.

---

[28] NCHE is a member of Southern Africa Quality Assurance Network (SAQAN) and African Qualifications Verification Network (AQVN). These initiatives seek to promote information sharing and harmonization of practices.

An informed student body and public are likely to make well informed decisions regarding which institution to go to and which programmes to pursue. Paradoxically, raising awareness has been resisted by some higher education institutions which thrive on ignorance of the students, guardians and the public about their legal standing, the quality of their programmes and above all their accreditation status. Some higher education institutions, public and private, have time and again attempted to challenge decisions in courts of law or lobbying for suspension of decisions that would presumably have adverse impacts on their public image, enrolment and profitability.[29]

Within the regulatory body non-compliance with the law can be a source of irreparable risk. The law provides for thirteen members of the Council, of which six are appointed in their personal capacity and seven are ex-officio members representing government departments, two vice chancellors representing public universities and one vice chancellor representing private universities. The argument over time has been the perceived under representation of private universities and colleges given that there are six public universities against an ever growing number of private universities, which exceed by far the number of public universities. Hence, the perception is that private universities operate in a legal environment founded on perceived bias and underrepresentation. The other four ex-officio members drawn from government ministries and departments are construed pro-public higher education institutions. The concern extends to considerations that the appointed members can become pro-public higher education institutions as well and position themselves as representatives of the public, not only in the statutory sense but also in their operational disposition such that private institutions' interests may not be handled impartially.

Contrary to the provisions in the constituting legislation, the first and second Councils were not gazetted per Section 4(4), a fact that haunted the second council, particularly in the months following the unfavourable Judicial Review of March 2018 to the reconstitution of the Council sometime later. Yet, subsequent

---

[29] Evidence on this matter is the court injunctions obtained by students and management of some private universities in 2016 and 2017. Although both court injunctions were vacated, a judicial review in one of the two cases succeeded on account that the appointment of the Council was not effected by publishing the names in the Malawi Government Gazettee.

appointments of the third and fourth councils in July 2018 and September 2020 did not respect the position of the law, where the correct reading is that appointments shall be made by the Minister. On each occasion questions that had arisen from stakeholders centred on the meaning of the 'government' and its personification with respect to the appointing powers or authority. Other questions have been on the actual composition of the council, including the suitability of appointees, as it has been felt by some stakeholders that appointments have never complied with the law and aspirations of higher education institutions; as a key stakeholder in the higher education regulation. For instance, some announcements have fallen short of mentioning the vice-chancellors designated to represent both public and private universities as was the case for the third council and the representative for private universities for the fourth council. It has also been felt that some appointees have been appointed to council despite not meeting qualities specified in Section 4 (1) (a) of the Act, which reads: "The Council shall consist of- a) six persons appointed by the Minister on account of high professional standing, special knowledge, skills and expertise in matters of higher education." Apparently, some key players in the higher education sector have tended to question the appointment not just on the basis of the law or merit of those appointed, but also on the extent to which the appointment reflect the understanding and expectations of those to be regulated. Another facet has been the term of office. The third council's term was curtailed before the end of the second year from the date of appointment and the curtailment coincided with the Fresh Presidential Elections (FPE) held in June 2020, which ushered into power a new administration. One of the decisions made then was the blanket dissolution of statutory boards. While the tenure of office is defined, including circumstances and factors that may affect the tenure of member of the Council, there is no provision for dissolution of the Council. This is evident from the reading of relevant sections on tenure of office, vacation of office of council member, and the provision on continuity of Council business. The provisions in reference read as follows:

> Section 5 (1) A member of the Council, other than an ex-officio member, shall hold office for a period of three years from the date of

appointment and shall be eligible for re-appointment at the expiry of that period:

Provided that non-ex officio members shall not be appointed for more than two consecutive terms of office.

Section 5 (2) on the expiry of the period for which an appointed member of the Council has been appointed, he shall continue to hold office until he has been re-appointed or a successor has been appointed:

Provided that a member shall not continue to hold office in terms of this subsection for more than six months.

Section 5 (3) When making any appointment after the expiry of the three years, the Minister shall have regard to the need to maintain a reasonable degree of continuity on the membership of the Council, so that at least half of the appointed members shall be re-appointed for the next term of office.

The sanctity of tenure of a member of the Council is provided in Section 5 (2) wherein it is apparent that expiry of three years specified in Section 5(1) is not a sufficient condition for the expiry of tenure of office. What completes tenure of office is re-appointment or appointment of a successor, or where re-appointment and appointment of successors have delayed, the expiry of six months following expiry of the three years as provided in 5(1). It follows that dissolution of the council by any authority could be illegal if provisions in Section 5 have not been complied with. This is true as section 6, which provides for vacation of office of members, does not provide for dissolution as a way by which a council member can cease to serve as its member. In particular, section 6 reads as follows:

The office of a member, other than an *ex officio* Member, shall become vacant –
  a) upon his death;
  b) if he had been absent from three consecutive meetings of the Council, of which he has had notice, without a reasonable cause;
  c) if he has been convicted of an offence without the option of a fine and sentenced to imprisonment for a period exceeding six months;

d) if he becomes mentally or physically incapable of efficiently performing his duties as a member of the Council; and
e) if he is adjudged bankrupt.

Further, Section 6(2) provides that a member may at any time resign his office by giving one month written notice to the Minister. The implications of dissolutions, where none of the above conditions have been satisfied should ordinarily raise questions, even calls for a judicial review in order to safeguard rule of law and perhaps curtail impunity in the governance of higher education regulatory processes. Besides exposing higher education regulation to political manipulation, it raises a fundamental question bordering on commitment to rule of law which is one of the globally recognised parameters of good governance. Its other parameters of interest are integrity, openness, transparency, accountability, participation. These parameters serve as yardsticks for appraising the traditions and institutions or how authority is exercised (Kaufmann et al, 2000) and it is also equally important as a discourse that emphasises the protection of the interests of the state and its subjects (Kaufmann and Kraay, 2003).

A regulatory framework that is founded on the principle of participation ought to manifest attributes of openness and representativeness. The shortfalls reflected above manifest non-compliance with respect to the law. A related matter is the absence of representation for the non-university higher education providers, those operating as colleges and institutes of management, among others. Absence of such representation will continue to make the regulatory regime pro-university in outlook besides being heavily pro-public entities. The anomaly is that to some stakeholder the regulatory regime is perceived to be unfriendly, that they may never get fair representation as they can never represent themselves or the universities, whether public or private. Even if they were, they would be devoid of legitimacy and therefore risk not being accepted as equals.

Higher education institutions

In the last twenty-five years, the higher education sector has been characterized by a rise from one to two, then three to four public universities and now six. The six public universities straddle a narrow range of programming including traditional areas of education and training in commerce, engineering, humanities, law, theology, science, nursing, medicine and social sciences. Besides the public universities, there are twenty private universities which outnumber the public universities by a ratio of 5:1. Ten (10) of the 20 private universities have been established by Christian Churches, reflecting the continuing significance of the influence of the Christian mission in the development and expansion of the education system in Africa. Many of the Christian universities have been established on premises that previously housed elementary, secondary or teacher training institutions and some have evolved out of ministerial training institutes, seminaries and colleges with an initial phase involving the upgrading of certificate and diploma programmes in theology and religious studies to degree level qualifications. These have been followed by the introduction of additional programmes in commerce, health and nursing education. An important trajectory is continuation of a commitment to serve for the betterment of humanity but also in response to government policy goals on access, equity, quality and relevance of higher education. The proliferation of private higher education provision is a recent development shaped by government's focus and policy on increasing access and to some degree quality, market relevance and good governance and management. In view of the provisions in the National Educational Sector Plan 2008 – 2017, ensuring and assuring quality is a call for greater and concerted commitment to the maintenance of a desired level of performance. In other words, increasing and widening access is not at odds with or should not be achieved at the expense of quality and relevance to the needs of society and the economy.

Private universities complement public institutions generally by contributing to widening of access to higher education. Some private institutions have through innovative programming increased the diversity of training programmes and flexible admission criteria broadened social participation. However, there have been increasing concerns about the quality of education and training, especially following the announcement by the National Council for Higher Education (NCHE) of accreditation results in 2016 and 2017, which showed that several private universities were operating below minimum standards. Recently, the concerns have been on what are considered to be non-meritorious doctoral awards to politically connected persons. These concerns reflect negatively on the credibility of private higher education institutions. As Alugbemiro Jegede (2012), former Secretary General of Association of African Universities, noted in his writing on the 'The Status of Higher Education in Africa', private universities experience the following challenges: shortage of resources, infrastructure and funds; over reliance on part-time staff from public universities and industry with implications both for the quality of delivery at the private universities and for effective performance in the public universities; concentration on directly marketable courses and programmes, thereby out-competing public universities; absence of research as a necessary part of the higher education enterprise; and exorbitant fees which keep out students from disadvantaged backgrounds. These challenges have serious impacts on the very need for increasing access and more importantly on quality of education and training as reflected above. Therefore, the challenges should be considered a call for progressive regulatory framework that includes evaluation of private universities and open and transparent systems for comparing and vetting qualifications earned from different institutions.

All higher education institutions have to be accredited by NCHE every seven years. New degree programmes created in the interim period must also undergo accreditation. The validity of the accreditation status of the institution depends on a positive outcome from the assessment and audit process. Among the many inputs, the single most important force for the maintenance of high quality in academic work lies in the close scrutiny and competitive review of candidates for employment, especially of lecturers. Lecturers are the key stakeholder in higher education given that higher education institutions have autonomy to plan, design, implement and evaluate their curricula and award qualifications. Therefore, those who teach, the lecturers and professors, are in essence the most important category of persons in curriculum implementation. Like teachers in primary and secondary education, the lecturers and professors have influence upon learners that cannot be measured precisely. Their influence extends beyond what goes on in the lecture room. Graduates who are retained as academics or who proceed into postgraduate training within or in other universities do carry with them the influence of their lecturers and professors and overtime such influence form a particular culture with a bearing on quality disposition beyond an institution. To inculcate a culture of quality and excellence, all higher education institutions (HEIs) should set up internal quality assurance systems and units with mandate for assuring the quality of teaching, research and community outreach. The units should assure quality while also contributing to the attainment of the founding mandate and performance objectives of each higher education institution.

Recently, it has been observed that providing quality education is a mammoth task for some private higher education institutions who are also struggling to comply with various statutory requirements, including employment elated laws. Some higher education institutions owe tax authorities and pension managers millions in arrears. Such indebtedness is an indication of governance and financial challenges, which if not addressed would have long term implications on the quality of education and the sustainability of higher education institutions. Therefore, as higher education institutions are investing in measures that support quality, there is also need to ensure compliance with relevant national laws.[30] Apparently institutions that have been non-compliant on quality issues tend to be non-compliant in other areas and with respect to their statutory obligations. Even those that are compliant on quality provision are in the long term likely to compromise on standards, especially where the need to settle the outstanding statutory obligations draw on and eventually drain resources earmarked and required for the maintenance of reasonable education standards and quality. Moreover, staff members retiring from non-compliant institutions are likely to suffer financial deprivation as a result of the non-compliance. The implications on those in the system could be less commitment to the institution and waste of time lost

---

[30] Following what sounded like 'name to shame' manner, among the non-compliant employers listed in 2019 by the Registrar of Financial Institutions were private higher education institutions such as Assemblies of God School of Theology (K20,330,496), Blantyre International University (K34,064,738.56), Daeyang Nursing College (K10,496, 742.30), ,and Daeyang University College of ICT (K7,050,254.37), Nkhoma University (K25,241,776.56), Pentecostal Life University (K7,327,234.20), Shareworld Open University (K3,312,292.50), Skyway University (K40,404,000), University of Livingstonia (K49,625,199.67)and Zomba Theological College (9,928,144.80). Apparently, the institutions had been in default for an extended period of 69,32,12,12,33,13,33,37,6,54 months respectively Source: *The daily Times*, August 19, 2019.

negotiating for better conditions with management by those serving as leaders in the trade union movement.

Students and alumni

As customers, students are the main consumer of higher education. Lecturers and professors are hired to teach the students. New knowledge and innovations are first and foremost presented to students and the consumption of which is intended to enrich and broaden the students' base of knowledge and skills. In customer theory, the customer is the final consumer in the chain of production. Chapleo and Simms (2010) have shown that although not the final consumer of the knowledge, skills and competences, students stand out as the primary (direct) customer of each higher education institution and secondarily (indirectly) the employer. The perceptions, needs and aspirations of students are therefore important markers of quality. Therefore, it is pertinent for quality assurance processes to pay attention to students' requirements and expectations, but also to their perceptions, how these perceptions are formed or changed and general understanding of quality education.

Apparently, the needs of the employer mean quite a lot in understanding the real needs of students. Equally important, the academic and career success of the graduates reflects the quality of education offered by the higher education institution that educated them. On one hand students tend to equate quality education to the quality of the academic experience, which reflects the academic rigour advanced by the academic staff as well as the overall situation of the teaching-learning experience. Hence, students expect to be taught and coached by academic staff who are experts, knowledgeable and acknowledged or referred scholarly authorities in their discipline, and who are also well equipped with necessary pedagogical skills. They expect the teachers to deliver content that is relevant to the needs industry and responsive to challenges in their society in an engaging and motivating way. Besides knowledge and skills, they seek enlightenment and inspiration. On the other hand, they are focused on the challenges ahead in the world of work, their employability and career development upon graduation. Put together, therefore, students' concerns in matters of quality assurance relate to:

- quality and relevance of the courses and programmes being delivered;
- availability and quality of the resources, technology and equipment that support the delivery of the courses;
- quality of the academic staff who are responsible for the design and sometimes review and delivery of the courses and programmes;
- quality, rigour and objectivity of assessment, and
- status of their institution in the rankings of quality.

The provision of quality education requires that the standard of entry into higher education should be at least comparable to the standard applicable to other reputable higher education institutions nationally and regionally. This calls for rigour in admission process. Students admitted should be those with requisite grades in their school leaving examinations and above average achievement in literacy and numeracy, critical thinking as well as problem solving. In the context of their higher education and training, the relationship between enrolment per programme and resources for their exclusive use in teaching and learning mean quite a lot in terms of quality and achievement of learning outcomes. It follows that if an institution admits under qualified students or has more students than they can be supported and attended to, the quality of teaching and learning support and output is likely to be compromised. The situation can be compared to the dilemma of feeding, dressing and accommodating a large population with meagre levels of productivity, which have long term negative implications on quality of life, productivity and ecological sustainability (Jimu 2016). So it is with education. Hence, this is a call for holistic approach to the question of quality; which is anchored by adequate student support services. Private funding for education in both public and private higher education institutions seems to be a critical challenge for some learners, mainly those from disadvantaged families. The challenges relate to meeting tuition and lodging fees which have been complicated by outsourcing of accommodation and catering services. Some students are compelled to withdraw for failure to pay tuition fees and lodging expenses.

The role of Industry and society

Industry and society at large benefit from human capital development anchored by higher education institutions. Graduates become employees, consumers and valuable members of society where they play various roles to advance the social, economic and political wellbeing. Therefore, quality higher education matters to both industry and society. Sometimes, however, higher education institutions have had difficulties relating with industry and communities. If community relations are neglected, the consequences tend to be severe for over a long period. Good neighbour, good deeds and effective public relations are all important in moulding positive engagement with industry and society.

Critical to industry and society is the quality of the programmes or research agenda of higher education institutions. Industry and community groups benefit more if they are involved in the development, resourcing, delivery, and review of the curriculum (Martin, 2000). Hence, for existing programmes regular review of the curriculum provides space for industry to continuously engage with the higher education institutions, to keep abreast with developments in the disciplines and contributing towards ensuring that curriculum is in sync with needs and trends in industry and society. Industry provides students valuable on-job and work-based learning opportunities. However, for industry and community to benefit to a significant extent it also depends on the quality of the students being accepted onto higher education courses and quality of instruction. With right inputs, the output is quality graduates produced under conditions that ensure that industry and society will derive maximum benefit.

Harmonizing expectations and responsibilities

From the analysis of the roles of the key stakeholders shared above it is evident that stakeholders in higher education have diverse stakes. Along the spectrum of stakes, some stakes are more personal, others formal and economic and yet others more political.

Different sets of interests and stakes apply at all levels and it is of paramount interest for quality assurance specialists and managers of higher education to know and work with stakeholders whose interests are varied and yet complementary, necessitating the need for better and greater understanding of interests that are likely to shape the policy discourse and the pursuit of quality education. It follows that beyond knowing the stakeholders through an identification process, higher education managers have a responsibility to learn and align diverse interests through good management decisions. This is necessary for effective and efficient management of quality assurance processes.

The state is a key stakeholder as a regulator regardless of whether that regulatory role is centralized or decentralized. Oftentimes the regulatory function includes determining and providing financing along with providing policy guidelines. Regulators have to grapple with a twin of concerns. On one hand, to be a vigilant enforcer of standards to prevent the proliferation of undeserving and substandard higher education institutions and programmes and on the other hand, to provide support to institutions and programmes which are failing to meet prescribed quality standards. It calls for empathy. Overtime, balancing the two imperatives provides regulators very narrow spaces for activity especially where higher education institutions are over-politicized, profit-oriented and the student body and their benefactors are either not well informed or are satisfied with mediocre provision. In such a situation management of higher education institutions, students and the public at large become accomplices in the watering down of quality. They react irresponsibly towards efforts to enforce a robust regulatory system and calls for accountability partly as a result of limited awareness of the intentions of the regulator.

Higher education institutions have the primary responsibility of responding to and being in sync with the requirements of a regulator in the interest of higher education beneficiaries, which include primarily the student and secondarily the employer and society at large. Being conversant with the regulatory standards is critical for seamless regulation. This includes an appreciation of conventional practices in higher education regulation founded on peer review mechanism. Hence, the use of expert peers implies that the regulatory practices are a shared concern and responsibility of stakeholders. Yet oftentimes this principle is missed in the discourse on higher education regulation especially where the role of peer reviewers is not well understood, sometimes subject to resistance, underplayed largely on account of uncompetitive ethic and mistrust among higher education institutions. The mistrust could arise from a lack of understanding over the standards and practices, for example, whether the peers will be applying standards prevailing within the institutions they are affiliated with or the national standards promulgated by the regulator. Sometimes, mistrust arises from a lack of confidence perpetuated by the insular and parochial approach to quality that institutions have maintained over time. The difference in terms of levels of development, experience and motivation to be regulated between public and private higher education institutions imply that discussions on quality tend to hinge on governance of quality in public institutions and adherence to quality in private institutions.

Turning to private higher education institutions, the profit motive may lead to serious compromises on the provision of an environment that is conducive to learning. Quality of infrastructure, availability of teaching and learning materials, quality and experience of teaching and support staff, admission processes and assessment of students may all be compromised in pursuit of profit. In order to have student numbers above the threshold, some institutions may admit unqualified students directly into degree and postgraduate programmes and yet others may introduce bridging course arrangements that do not meaningfully address the pre-entry gaps. The teaching, learning and assessment standards may be watered down further to a level where those who were unqualified in the first place graduate with first class or distinction. The drive to accommodate those with ability to pay overriding merit may facilitate the watering down of standards. In both public and private institutions, the ability to pay is overshadowing quality as institutions seek to sustain revenue flows from fee paying students. However, where the pursuit of quality is a facet of institution culture, as higher education institutions are responding to the needs of the primary and secondary stakeholders in this sense, they in turn become intertwined with different sets of stakeholders such as suppliers of teaching and learning materials, providers of ancillary services such as security, cleaning, communication, water and electricity, civic groups, among others. The economic, social and political interests of these service providers and civic groups become closely linked to the needs of the students and the industry and the quality assurance regime.

It is pertinent that at all times and in all circumstances that higher institutions have and must endeavour to meet the needs of their students, teaching staff and other employees. The category employee is inclusive as it covers everyone from the security person stationed at the entrance gate to the office assistant who delivers mail or serve tea, and the administrators and managers of units that provide support services. Higher education institutions have to strive to satisfy the needs of every member of staff considering that they have a role in the provision of quality higher education. Besides meeting the needs of the internal constituency, there is also a need to look out for the needs and interests of external stakeholders. For instance, in order to maintain consistent enrolment, higher education institution must connect with prospective students, parents and teachers in the secondary schools and the media. In their dealing with staff and student issues higher educations have a duty of ensuring that the needs of the rest of the stakeholders are also satisfied. They have to ensure that their operations are in sync with the requirements of external funding agencies that support students through scholarships and grants for fees and research. Proper alignment of the curricula to needs of the labour market needs not emphasizing. Another important area is financing higher education through public-private partnerships (PPP), whereby private businesses and companies or investors commit resources towards infrastructure development projects such as academic facilities (lecture theatres, science laboratories, libraries, ICT infrastructure), student and faculty housing, and other facilities on higher education campuses. On-going PPPs in some public universities have focused solely on expansion of student accommodation on build-operate-transfer (BOT) arrangement because there is a direct benefit in form of profit from renting out accommodation units to students until the facilities could be transferred to the institutions.

The pursuit for continuous engagement of the multistakeholdership is necessary if the higher education sector is to register progress and achieve not just the much needed effective regulation but also to build a common understanding of quality and academic excellence that is expected. Given the experiences, needs and expectations of different stakeholders, quality assurance stretches beyond meeting minimum requirements and interests of particular stakeholder group. It entails a dialogue among stakeholders, setting meaningful standards and expectations. That includes pursuit for excellence in infrastructure, governance, programming, teaching and learning, assessment, research, engagement with industry and society at large. Each facet presents a unique set of opportunities. Benchmarking stakeholder involvement is also critical issue. For Elmuti and Kathawala (1997), benchmarking is the process of identifying the highest standards of excellence and then making the improvements necessary to reach those standards, commonly called "best practices". It is a way of discovering what is the best performance being achieved, whether in a particular institution, by a competitor or by an entirely different industry. This information can then be used to identify gaps in an organization's processes in order to attain competitive advantage. It requires ongoing and systematic measuring and comparing of the work processes of an organization along fundamental performance issues articulated by the following questions (Prasad and Stella (n.d.):[31]

a) Are we performing better than we have ever performed?
b) Are there any other organizations that are performing well and from whom we can learn?
c) Are there any practices that will improve our performance?

Active stakeholder engagement in benchmarking is therefore a strategic management tool that higher education institutions may not do without to enhance the quality of their programme offerings. This is true given that benchmarking covers aspects of planning, facilitates the setting of organisational goals, measuring of productivity, and making effective comparisons on the basis of best practices. Therefore, it is also true to state that benchmarking stakeholder involvement can be used as a point of reference to achieve quality, efficiency and effectiveness. Three forms of benchmarking can be deduced: process benchmarking to achieve quality output, performance benchmarking to realize economies of efficiency and strategic benchmarking to improve on effectiveness.

---

[31] Prasad, V S and Stella, A. (n.d.) "Best Practices Benchmarking in Higher Education for Quality Enhancement", *Best Practices in Higher Education*. http://naac.gov.in/docs/Best%20Practices/Best%20Practise%20in%20Higher%20Education.pdf

A point to be emphasized is that through effective stakeholder engagement, higher education institutions can better achieve and also guarantee quality education today, tomorrow and in the future. Achieving quality through a calculated stakeholder engagement will assure institutions of achieving their goals, marketing their brand and securing their reputations. It is also pertinent to note that to gain accreditation some standards and guidelines require stakeholder participation. Hence, who is participating and how is participation structured, measured and accounted for should continue to influence perceptions and articulations of quality in higher education. It follows that higher education institutions may not skirt around the need to satisfy their stakeholder interests if they are to remain relevant and compliant with quality standards as well.

It is conventional wisdom that the primary responsibility for assuring quality of higher education rests with the higher education institutions. Once an institution is established, in terms of primacy of responsibility and accountability for the quality and relevance of the education offered; management, staff and students of each higher education institution should take a lead and shoulder the responsibility and burden of ensuring that standards are upheld. The role of the policy holder, the industry, and other higher education institutions and of course the regulatory/governing bodies should be to complement by way of validation of the internal quality assurance processes. Also, if higher education institutions are to be agents for change, there is a need for effective measures to address challenges of inadequate infrastructure (lecture theatres, hostels for student accommodation) and teaching and learning materials. It is also necessary to correct challenges posed by underfunding and mismanagement. Every higher education institution should have a well-defined mission and vision that are understood by all stakeholders. Every institution should have clearly defined framework of quality. A well-functioning monitoring system is also critical for the good governance and management.

There is a need to rethink the relationship between stakeholders, and more importantly one between higher education institutions, the government and governance institutions established for the higher education sector. From the NESP, it was noted that challenges to higher education are somehow due to restrictive statutory prescriptions, public policy vacuum and opaque relationship between higher education institutions with the government (Ministry of Education, Science and Technology, 2008). The establishment of additional higher education institutions (both public and private) and the operational mundus of governing bodies such as NCHE and HESLGB have exposed various areas requiring immediate action. For instance, the harmonization of selection of students has created perceptions of an erosion of the autonomy of the governing councils of public universities to determine criteria and select students as they would if the regulatory regime had not been revised without taking full account of the autonomy that such institutions have to exercise. Where the regulator is actually involved in activities and processes beyond setting and monitoring of standards, perceptions of bias may, even if unfounded, appear credible. The requirement that private higher education institutions should be registered by the Council while public universities may not, imply double standards as some public institutions may begin or continue offering programmes even if they do not meet the minimum requirements. Also, the delinking of admission of students from student financing has exposed deserving students from disadvantaged backgrounds to incessant pressures of not being able to meet tuition and accommodation support from the state. The requirement that institutions (both public and private) should vet student loan applicants, places training institutions in very awkward situations where students certified as needy have to be expected to meet their fee obligation despite being unable to access a loan from the state. The other gap has been the absence of overarching policy direction for the higher education sector, which means that some legislative reforms have been pursued piecemeal, sometimes without effective consultations, and in a rather haphazard manner. The now defunct equitable selection of students to public universities is perhaps the most well-known example.

At one time urban centres of Mzuzu, Lilongwe, Zomba and Blantyre were for the purpose of student admission to public universities treated as standalone districts. A policy position that was initially conceived to apply to the one and only university at the time was eventually extended to all other public universities that emerged later as if the assumptions that informed the policy had not changed, and oblivious of the resistance to its implementation within the public universities and from the general public. Within the public universities the key concern was one of merit and the dilemma of selecting students with lower grades instead of those with excellent grades for the sake of being politically correct. The neglect of merit in favour of pseudo equity was perhaps a scar that made equitable access such a dreaded phenomenon. The fall of quota, as it were, has not addressed fully the opaque relationship between higher education institutions and the government, not only with respect to the perspective of the older higher education institution but also with respect to the new ones, and the regulatory bodies. Again, weaknesses and deficiencies in public university management system, for instance, absence of clear regulations governing processes such as the creation of teaching posts, appointment of staff, the tenure system, monitoring of productivity, staff absenteeism (Ministry of Education, Science and Technology, 2008) and the determination of available space or in-take have remained unattended to thereby affecting negatively commitments to improve access and enhance quality and relevance of higher education from the public higher education perspective. It follows that there is need for an integrated approach based in effective participation of key stakeholders.

Conclusion

This chapter has demonstrated the importance of stakeholder analysis to achieve effective implementation of programmes, improve governance and quality in higher education, mainly public higher education. It has elaborated on the opportunities, constraints and the future directions for effective stakeholder engagement. The urgency of involved stakeholdership has also been demonstrated. The discussion presents a strong case for more reflective and involved stakeholder engagement, effective planning and design of academic programmes, and monitoring and evaluation of quality assurance processes.

Chapter 4

Operating Context and Quality Culture in the Private Higher Education Subsector

Introduction

Most private higher education institutions, universities in particular, are new, established in the last decade and in the process of setting up and consolidating management and governance systems. Most are small in terms of infrastructure and facilities, enrolment, the range of programmes and staff capacity. Key among the challenges to date has been ensuring that governance and management systems are functioning well and that academic processes and awards or qualifications can be enhanced and trusted. A corresponding set of aspects is therefore one of ensuring appropriate quality standards, procedures and practices are in place, functioning and producing expected results. This chapter will focus on the operational context and quality culture through a focus on staffing issues, terms and conditions of service, leadership and sustainability from the financial point of view.

Operating context

Among the three pillars for higher education, it appears that the wish to increase access has been the fundamental tenet for the rise of private higher education institutions. The perceptions that there is generally a big gap of access, that there is a segment of the population whose interests and needs are not being addressed or receiving adequate attention and that the demand for higher education is higher than the capacity of public institutions have been used to justify the opening of more private colleges, business schools and universities. Private colleges and business schools and some private universities offer mostly franchise programmes in collaboration with and on behalf of business schools in the United Kingdom.[32] Therefore, the need to respond to specific needs of

---

[32] Key qualifications are from institutions in United Kingdom such as Association of Certified Chartered Account (ACCA), Association of Business Executives (ABE), Association of Business Managers and Administrators

some secondary school leavers, the internationalization of learning through open, distance, and online learning and the rise of cross-border provisioning of tertiary education have all played a part. Hence, a major contribution of private higher education institutions to education and society has been their contribution to the widening of access of tertiary education. Other dimensions are innovative programming, diversity of training programmes and flexible admission criteria which have broadened inclusion, and enhanced the participation of mature entry students who had no opportunity to attend postsecondary education in their youth or those who just want to upgrade or acquire new qualifications and skills.

Besides the immense contribution towards expanding access, they have raised awareness that it possible to run programmes with little or no infusion of state funding. The governance and management model, which in some cases represent a complete departure from the prevailing governance forms in public institutions have also informed a discourse on how to streamline and realigned governance and management practices in public institutions. On the other hand there have been concerns about the quality of education and training offered by some private institutions, those offering their own programmes and qualifications, especially following the announcement by the NCHE of first accreditation results in 2016/17, which showed that several private universities were operating below minimum standards. Then, all private higher education institutions that had passed and attained accreditation were accredited with conditions, suggesting that there was greater room for improvement of their programmes and operating context. Despite that some of the institutions that had lost accreditation then have regained it in subsequent assessments; there are lingering gaps, if not doubts, about the capacity of some, but also their commitment to excellence. The COVID 19 situation has exposed many institutions to new challenges, one of which is that it has amplified the question of quality juxtaposed with that of financial sustainability. Many private institutions have since 2020 adopted blended learning using various online platforms for which they were unprepared.

(ABMA) and Chartered Institute of Procurement and Supply (CIPS), just to mention some.

The magnitude of the contribution of private higher education institutions is that at least sixteen private universities are accredited and over twenty-five are registered as of 2021. As pointed out in the first chapter, private higher education institutions can be categorized into church affiliated institutions and non-church affiliated institutions. This distinction is important to the extent that it amplifies the historical reality of the introduction of western schooling in Malawi and also the operational and governance realities of the private higher education sub-sector. The historical reality is that formal schooling was a private initiative of early Christian Missionaries from the last quarter of the 19th Century and since then the church has been a key provider of education at all levels. However, the church's influence in higher education gained momentum after 2000 and this development and coincidence is strongly associated with the liberalizations in the economic and political spheres in the mid-1990s. Catholic, Protestant and Pentecostal churches have a fair presence in the private higher education space.[33] Other private establishments, because of the way they were established or operate, appear to family based,[34] and yet to break from the founder syndrome.

Most of the new private universities operate in rented premises. Most of the premises were not purposely built for the provision of higher education and training. For a developing country with a small and less vibrant construction sector, suitable space is not readily available. Hence, another key feature of private higher education provisioning is the prevalence of improvisation in teaching and learning spaces and even so in the administrative

---

[33] Catholic universities include the Catholic University of Malawi and DMI St John the Baptist University. The Church of Central Africa Presbyterian operates three universities under its three synods; namely: University of Livingstonia, Nkhoma University and University of Blantyre Synod. Universities associated with Pentecostal Churches are Malawi Assemblies of God University and Pentecostal Life University. Other church affiliated institutions are African Bible College, Daeyang University, Malawi Adventist University and Lake Malawi Anglican University. Almost all (the exception being the University of Blantyre Synod) commenced their operations prior to 2015.

[34] In this category are Blantyre International University, Shareworld Open University, Exploits University, Skyway University, Millennium University, Jubilee University, Hebron University, Marble Hill University and the now defunct institutions (Riverton University, Columbia Commonwealth University and Africa University of Guidance, Counselling and Youth Development). Most of these institutions started operating after 2015.

arrangements. Many entities have challenges with providing adequate learning space and facilities, laboratories and library facilities commensurate with their programme needs. Besides the challenge of under investment in infrastructure, some manifest lack of a culture of openness, accountability, transparency and integrity. Many are constrained in their capacity to recruit, train and retain qualified academic staff. The primary challenge has been limited financial capacity and limited pool of qualified candidates on the market.[35]

Staff issues and terms and conditions of service

Since 2016 one of the key issues that have affected accreditation of some private institutions or programme has been understaffing or unqualified staff. Coincidentally, during the first round of assessment for accreditations, only one private university reported providing support for doctoral training and none provided grants to support research. The situation has since improved. Yet, the underlying challenge remains unresolved.

Many private universities experience challenges meeting their financial obligations to both teaching and non-teaching staff. One of the implications is inability to provide terms and conditions of service that can support the need to recruit and retain well qualified and competent staff at all levels. This challenge has been compounded by the competition for staff, where the most qualified, experienced and therefore competent personnel are in high demand and the turnover rate for such cadre of staff has been relatively high. While this trend stands to benefit institutions with more sustainable funding mechanisms and strong reputations, the implication on the sector as a whole could be rated negative if perceived from the underdevelopment and underperforming of new and developing institutions due to loss of staff. Over time there have been significant losses of staff from some private to public universities, from some private universities to other private universities; a situation to be observed in the public higher education space, where the movement has been from the old to the

---

[35] Per Minimum Standards for Higher Education, for degree granting institutions being qualified implies possession of academic qualification of at least master's or equivalent. Those without master's qualification may be engaged as interns or staff development fellows.

new institutions but also from colleges of education that are directly controlled by the state to semi-autonomous public universities. In a space of five or more years, public colleges of education have lost many well trained staff soon after the staff returned from further training within Malawi or from abroad, where they were supported to pursue either masters or doctoral training, and the loss has been to other public institutions. The major attraction has been higher than average remuneration offered at public universities. The staff, having served a minimum number of years required for voluntary or early retirement from civil service, opts for early exit to join public or private universities where they take up tenured employment with contributory pension or fixed term employment contracts that provide either gratuity or contributory pension and in some cases both. Therefore, the disparity in wages within the higher education sector and between public institutions stands out as a major factor affecting retention of staff.

As expected for a liberalized economy, terms and conditions of service would vary from one institution to another. However, in some institutions the terms and conditions tend to be imprecise, contentious and less attractive. Among the private entities the variations reflect financial sustainability, age and proprietorship. There are major variations between new and older institutions, and church affiliated and non-church affiliated institutions. Institutions in the former category mostly operate on non-profit/pro-service terms, while the latter are for profit. While most church owned institutions have a relatively larger pool of permanent staff engaged on fixed term contract and with defined terms of tenure, most non-church affiliated institutions have few full-time staff. In that case most of the full time staff works in administrative positions. Often, family members form the bulk of administrative staff. Some sit on the governing boards and others combine both administration and teaching roles. Non-family staff members (those not related by blood to the proprietor) are either on part-time terms and where they are on full-time or fixed contract terms, their terms of engagement are nonetheless precarious. Some contracts are convenient and cosmetic arrangements that fuel unfair labour practices besides those relating to governance and management per se. This is true for low level staff and high level staff alike as cases of lack of tenure security, high turnover and frequent dismissal of Vice-Chancellors in some private institutions would suggest.

Some Vice-Chancellors have been unable to serve for a full term of one to three years. Some have been forced to resign or risk dismissal for unsubstantiated allegations of incompetence and yet others for allegedly promoting financial prudence, for example, spending within budget against the wishes of the proprietors, prioritizing debt repayment and compliance with statutory provisions on tax and pension or for ensuring that the institution has resources that are exclusively dedicated to the education and training function as required by law. This aspect is a particular trait for some private institutions. The trait suggests the need for a different model, guidelines and code of conduct for leadership in private universities and colleges.

Terms and conditions of employment may be framed providing for a range of benefits for staff such as salary, medical and pension cover and duty facilitating allowances for those performing administrative responsibilities such as serving as head of department or dean of faulty or school. More often than not, due to cash flow constraints, in reality the statutory provisions on tax and pension are rarely complied with and stipulated allowances are paid only when it is convenient. The paradox is that those holding senior leadership positions and therefore strategically placed to formulate policy and steer implementation have been ineffective at implementing meaningful terms and conditions of service appropriate to the mission and reasonable expectations for the sector. This explains why some institutions fair low in terms of being able to recruit and retain qualified staff as stated above. It explains why some private institutions have had their accreditation withdrawn at some point in time for failing to maintain reasonable standards, and also the tendency of some institutions to seek reliefs from courts instead of addressing recommendations for improvement so that they are compliant with respect to minimum standards.

Leadership and institutional sustainability

While it is possible for institutions to succeed when leadership is lacking, it is difficult to imagine an institution with effective administration and good employee relationships without stable and effective leadership. In other words, leadership matters and effective management and governance require that there should be effective leadership. Lack of stability at leadership level is a red flag.

Some private universities have changed proprietorship and others the leadership more than once in a space of a few years. Leaders who have failed to bring profit or secure accreditation for some institutions have not been spared, even where the causes for underperformance have been underinvestment by proprietors and lack of oversight by boards and trustees. . Yet, in other institutions, those who compromise on national quality indicators have survived in cases where the underperformance in quality did not translate into significant financial losses. These may include instances where enrolment was enhanced by recruiting students who barely met admission criteria and sometimes graduating students with incomplete academic records as a means of attracting more students. In such situations managers and staff who speak out against unconventional practices may be labelled difficult and enemies of the institutions. In other instances, the leadership may introduce more programmes and enrol more students despite serious shortfalls in staff capacity. In order to gain registration for new programmes or accreditation for old programmes, records of staff may be falsified to disguise the inadequacy in their state of preparedness. Such acts, though they manifest lack of integrity, have never been sanctioned from within. Some institutions have treated the reporting of such weaknesses (even if uncovered by external reviewers) as a form of external intrusion into their operations facilitated by insiders to sabotage the institutions. On the contrary is a dent on leadership that thrive on misinformation and dishonesty.

Leadership quality has implications on institutional sustainability. Where it is missing, coupled with financial challenges, there is a grave risk of institutions failing to continue operating efficiently or risk closing abruptly in some cases. Some may descend into diploma mills. The institution that was deregistered in 2016 and then re-registered in 2018 under a different name is a case in point. Following its re-assessment for re-registration, it emerged that that institution had huge unsettled rental arrears. Apparently, the institution was heavily indebted and its debts included unpaid personal emoluments for lecturers. For a while the institution had its assets temporarily bequeathed to another institution. Soon after obtaining re-registration the leadership organised a swift return to the previous premises and a graduation ceremony for students;

some of which were politically exposed persons (PEP). There were allegations of ghost students who graduated with first class/distinction. The implication is that quality compromises may provide a festering environment in which some institutions operate as diploma mills; understood as institutions that peddle academic and professional qualifications (Jimu 2018).

It appears that building capacity to set up and maintain appropriate governance and operational systems are daunting challenges. Defining requirements and expecting institutions to comply is also not enough. Policing the operations of institutions is a necessary evil. This is true for many institutions where availability of policies, systems and even structures has little bearing on implementation of appropriate academic and human resource processes and practices. Provisions at policy level are intended to meet and satisfy external regulatory requirements than to effectively guide internal governance and practice.

A point to emphasize is that governance and operational limitations stem from two fronts; failure to set up and operate an efficient bureaucratic system and failure to mobilise adequate resources. Yet in some instances, it appears that the bureaucratic inertia is compounded by the lack of experience and awareness of business processes appropriate for effective running of higher education. Founders, proprietors and even trustees of some institutions have been people of modest education and training. Some have no experience in higher education matters, yet others appear to be lacking in proper orientation and values. No wonder some institutions have part-time leadership at vice chancellor level. Some appoint or solicit services of persons with strong academic or administration profiles gained in the public higher education sector or civil service only to serve as titular or nominal heads, while others less qualified and inexperienced manage operations on day to day basis. That is, title holders are figureheads devoid of any significant influence in areas that matter, that is, policy and strategic direction, institutional sustainability and quality enhancement.

For the non-church affiliated institutions, the challenge has a different manifestation. The tendency has been to place a multitude of family members in strategic governance and management positions regardless of their suitability in terms of qualifications and experience. These incestuous arrangements imply that key decisions, for instance, planning and budgeting, hiring of leadership, procurement of assets, and organisation and performance of ceremonies in the university or college are family affairs. Key decisions may be made outside formal structures of the university. Non-family members working for the institutions, regardless of the rank that they may hold in the institutional set up, become spectators, while others operate merely as co-opted and unwilling participants in academic and non-academic processes. The credibility and integrity of awards from institutions with such governance and management arrangements may not pass a credibility test.

The goal of financial sustainability has been hard to attain for various reasons. Most private universities depend on tuition fees for all their operational costs. Without going into the details, it is pertinent to mention that unit costs vary from institution to institution and year to year. Such costs have been shown to be very high for Malawi compared to other countries, and that they are much higher for public higher education institutions than private institutions (The World Bank, 2010:165 for an earlier account). Science, engineering and medical programmes are relatively more expensive to run than business, accounting, social science and arts/humanities programmes. Major contributors to cost of running programmes are requirements such as infrastructure and equipment for laboratories and workshops, and staff costs such as remuneration and welfare. Underinvestment in sciences and overreliance on part-time arrangements could account for patterns in unit costs in private higher education institutions.

Private higher education institutions that have alternative sources of financing are few and such sources do not constitute a significant proportion of their operating budgets. With budgets tied to tuition, failure to collect tuition fees has been recipe for underinvestment in infrastructure and equipment, salaries that fall short of incentivizing staff and underinvestment in research and development. For church linked institutions, some receive contributions from the parent church, congregations and partners from the developed world. The general rule has been the university or college should be able to generate adequate income and support its operations entirely from tuition fees. In some cases, the university is considered a strategic business unit of the parent church, from which the church can draw support and sustenance financially. The financial underperformance of such a university implies serious expectations gap in the church and the implication has been dwindling resource for the effective operation of the university and non-effectiveness of its financial governance. The levels of remuneration for staff have been kept low, aligned to those in allied church institutions than those within the higher education sector. Capacity building through training and research has also suffered from gross underfunding.

In non-church affiliated private higher education institutions the expectation and pursuit for profit maximization has sometimes led to various compromises including hiring of persons that are not only unqualified but also uncommitted to anchor the profit maximization agenda. The perception that one can make profit from low investment has led to the situation where some proprietors and management of some private higher education institutions have taken advantage of the public's desperation for higher education by offering substandard education in facilities or using equipment that do not reflect well on the mission of higher education. In extreme cases of desperation, to gain accreditation some private higher education institutions have resorted to misrepresentation of information about their financial position, programmes and staff complement. Other institutions have also hired laboratory equipment, computers, books and fire extinguishers just to show off and stage quality ostensibly to gain registration or accreditation. The challenges are that entities that are not ready to roll-out or continue offering programmes get registered or accredited thereby rendering the regulatory regime ineffective.

Some institutions attract many students through what are known as degree completion programmes, where persons with certificates and diplomas, regardless of the quality and credibility of the awarding bodies have been admitted to third or final year of study of four year degree programmes and yet they are often required to pay module exemption fees for all the modules that have been waived. Notwithstanding the merits of recognition of prior learning and multiple entry-multiple exit arrangements, which have become acceptable practice from the point that as they promote life-long learning, the name degree completion is misleading and a marketing gimmick as it emphasises the acquiring of certificate as opposed to pursuit of meaningful learning, education and training. The students enrolled on degree completion have their attention set on obtaining a degree, and not on the transformation that is envisaged in the process of earning the degree. Hence, degree completion debases and trivializes the good intentions of human capital development experts who have been promulgating for multiple entry and multiple exit and exemptions based on equivalence of demonstrated prior leaning. Degree completion is a money making syndicate, where 'money for credits' appears to be the rule. Yet, to graduate from such programmes students are further asked to pay substantial sums for hiring academic dress and for venue costs. Payment for the knowledge not imparted by the institution and for the celebration of learning that has not been achieved is a gross form of credentialism. Some graduation ceremonies are therefore displays of mediocrity and mischief given that some graduates cannot demonstrate the level of learning being recognized through concocted graduation ceremonies. The paradox is that employers and society are given a raw deal thanks to the mal-governance that has allowed for growth of institutions that provide for admission of persons to programmes they are not qualified for, those who are already in employment and provided they have capacity to pay the unwarranted fees. Such students can afford the luxury of hiring cheating consultants who do everything for them including writing assignments and research projects on their behalf. These situations are compounded by a combination of lowly paid and poorly motivated teaching staff and time constraints affecting attendance at lectures. Assigning others to do assignments and reports imply that the quality of some graduates becomes wanting, hence the tragedy of credentialism (Jimu 2018).

Conclusion

This chapter has focused on the operational context and credibility of some private higher education institutions. Provision and management of appropriate infrastructure, systems and processes, and human resource adequate for the mission of higher education are some of the issues that require serious consideration. Poor governance is manifested by the insensitivity of institutions to the need to provide appropriate facilities and equipment and guarantee adherence to employment and labour related laws, respect for set human resource and administrative arrangements and commitment to the sustainability of the institution. It follows that enhancing the governance regime will require institutional commitment to effective operationalization of processes appropriate for the development of a well-regulated higher education. Increasing access should be pursued judiciously in order to avoid the widening gap between increasing access and quality. As Alugbemiro Jegede (2012), former Secretary General of Association of African Universities, noted writing on the 'The Status of Higher Education in Africa', private higher education institutions should work towards addressing operational challenges, which include the following:

a) Shortage of resources, infrastructure and funds;
b) Over reliance on part-time staff mostly from public universities with implications both for the quality of delivery at the private universities and for effective performance in the public universities;
c) Absence of research funding as a necessary part of the higher education enterprise; and
d) Exorbitant fees which keep out deserving students from disadvantaged backgrounds.

The challenges stated above, if they remain unaddressed for prolonged time, have serious on the very need for increasing access and more importantly on the need to enhance quality. Further, as observed by Oduaran and Oduaran (2005) it is clear that addressing the gaps requires right inputs (good physical infrastructure, qualified teachers and instructional materials) and right processes (effective management, effective teaching/learning and assessment) in order to have right outputs. Private higher education institutions should continue mobilising resources towards infrastructure development, procurement of teaching and learning materials, staff remuneration, training and research. There is need for a progressive regulatory framework that includes regular monitoring and audits of higher education institutions focusing on their commitment to continuous improvement and quality culture.

Chapter 5

Peer Review as a Quality Control Process

Introduction

The term "peer" is derived from the Latin "par' for "equal". Therefore, to be a peer is to be an equal to another person per set criteria. For instance, academic qualifications, professional standing, and social status have been used as yardsticks for determining peers from this literal sense. The term peer-review brings into focus a certain form of relationship between those considered to be peers; a relationship that involves evaluation, and hence it conveys a particular form of potential evaluation carried out by another person, for example, an academic or academics, usually in the same discipline (Kis 2005). In the terms of Wilger (1997) peer review denotes the involvement of external professionals in making judgments, evaluations and decisions about proposals for new academic programmes, the continuation or modification of existing programmes, the quality of research programmes, or the quality of institutions. From the understanding provided above it can be inferred that the term peer reviewer refers to a person conducting peer reviews. However, it is important to add that peer review should also be understood as a methodology dominant in research evaluation but also one that is increasingly used in the evaluation of the quality of teaching and learning (Kis 2005)... It has been effective for hundreds of years and as Slyvia Wicks (1992) put it then, it has qualities that make it suitable for at least the next twenty five years. That peer review has outlived the projected years suggests that it is a reliable and perhaps robust and dynamic methodology.

Biagioli (2002) noted that, in terms of origin, peer review dates back to the rise of the book publishing industry in the seventeenth century. Journal publishers implemented reviews at a later stage. Pontille and Torny (2014), for instance, linked peer review to mid-twentieth-century changes to academic structures, situating the concept of anonymous peer review to 1955, with the American Sociological Review's 'experiment in evaluation' which was later popularised by other journals. The use of 'single blind', 'double blind', and 'open review' models in journal reviews were introduced much later in the 1980s and their expanded use was recorded in the mid-1990s. However, Kennison (2016) observed a direct link between peer review practices and changes to the structure and funding of higher education institutions such that peer review became the norm during the rapid growth in higher education after World War II and the concurrent explosion in Cold War driven research funding. To date peer reviews are quite common and therefore a fundamental practice, for example, in scientific and referred journals; research funding agencies; academic conferences (that is peer review or evaluation of abstracts and chapters for conferences); and book publishers, just to cite a few examples. Peer reviewers are expected to contribute to maintenance of standards; improvement of performance, guarantee credibility of processes and output, provide accurate feedback, reliable and well-grounded advice and decisions. Peer review decisions may range from "accept", "accept with revisions" or "reject".

Objectivity of the process anchors its integrity. Integrity is a buzzword in higher education as it attests to the sincerely and fairness of academic systems, processes and procedures. Integrity requires that the peer review process is conducted by experts who are also committed to the values of scholarship, its progress, transparency, professionalism and accountability. Hence, the reviewers should be persons who are well acquainted with developments in their field of specialization. Being experts with a flavour of professionalism and accountability are ingredients for credible peer review process and sustenance of public trust. Professionalism engenders open and honest dialogue between scholars and administrators that are involved, providing also space for further learning, innovation and open sharing of ideas among peers. The result may be tacit and objective external supervision, sufficient internal control, and horizontal accountability. As a form of citizen centred governance of higher education, it mitigates institutional and market failures. To that extent Mario Biagioli described peer review as probably the most distinctive feature of the modern academic system in the sense that it sets academics apart from all other professions by construing value through peer judgment, not market dynamics or purely state control. Yet, he also observed that there is so little research that has analysed it empirically or philosophically to the extent that reflections on peer review have often been confined to private conversations or treated as one of the practical aspects of the profession rather than as an intellectual subject (Biagioli, 2002).

The use of peer review and its implications for quality control manifest the uniqueness of higher education, especially the enormity of the responsibility and trust placed upon the teachers and managers of higher education institutions to provide quality education with minimal external and often in a decentralized framework of control. As stated earlier higher education institutions retain the autonomy to determine what to teach (curriculum), how to teach it, how to assess and also certify the level of learning and training achieved. That universities and colleges world over from antiquity have enjoyed an array of liberties testify to the uniqueness of the character of higher education as a distinct realm. Such a realm should not be completely devoid of normative standards for conducting such reviews.

Peer review as a tool in quality assurance

In many of the world's higher education regulatory regimes, registration and accreditation of institutions and programmes stand out as fundamental processes through which the regulatory function is exercised. Predefined and widely agreed minimum standards provide a framework for what is expected of higher education providers as they set up or continue to offer programmes and award qualifications. Registration is fundamentally a process through which prospective higher education providers showcase their state of readiness and to that effect peer review would focus on assessing the provisions and availability of conditions necessary for the launching of an institution and its programmes. Upon being authorized to set up, preparations for accreditation and subsequent assessment would focus on the maintenance of appropriate standards, systems and processes. Hence, at registration the prospective institution would commit to set up in a manner that provide conditions fit for purpose, showcasing infrastructure, programmes, policies and human resource requirements. The question is how to assess and validate the provisions and commitments for the purpose of delivering quality and relevant education? Further, prospective higher education institutions have to demonstrate from the start their commitment to quality and excellence by meeting the necessary conditions required for the realization of the quality agenda. In a practical sense peer reviews would be expected to provide external, third party, independent as well as objective insight into the higher education provision (Ryan 2015). Hence, the peer review process serves as a quality control process, a means for measuring excellence and value, confirmation of consistency, and gauging whether and the extent to which expectations of the clientele will be met. The next question becomes how should peer review be structured, including the selection of peer reviewers?

Peer reviewers should be suitably qualified, which is understood as possession of minimum academic qualification of master's level from an accredited higher education institution. Ideally, peer reviewers are expected to be senior enough within the higher education set-up, which is interpreted as having attained the rank of at least senior lecturer/senior administrator. Benchmarking of peer review processes is critical. Following on the practice in the United States, peer review teams include faculty and administrative peers in the profession and they are involved for reviewing the self-study and in conducting site visits (Eaton 2004 cited in Kis 2005). Informed by Danish quality assurance practice, the review team may also include non-academic public members who have an interest in higher education (Thune 1998 cited in Kis 2005) Demonstrable knowledge of programme design, content and pedagogy is expected of academic reviewers. However, possession of attributes mentioned above does not qualify a person to be a peer reviewer. Those who are deemed qualified require induction/ training focusing on the philosophy of external quality assurance, methods and methodology for conducting assessments. Then assessments can be conducted by way of inspection of infrastructure, facilities and equipment; conducting interviews with staff and students; and reviewing policy, curricula or programme documents and records. Peer reviewers are further expected to assess programmes and so an understanding of developments in broad and specific disciplines and fields of scholarship is required. Equally important is ability to validate self-assessment reports, attention to details required for checking and confirming relevance of information and evidence and ability to identify and unravel misrepresentations, appraise strengths, weaknesses and make suggestions or recommendations in alignment to areas for improvement that are grounded in factual information generated in the conduct of the inspection and review, supported by best evidence available, external reference points such as guidelines, standards and relevant legislation and policies. The array of skills and competences justify a robust screening process of reviewers. Where screening is absent or inadequate; many challenges may arise including concerns of lack of legitimacy, integrity and even the credibility of decisions.

Reviewers may be withdrawn from participating in an assessment on account that they do not possess one or the other set of competences or for being considered relatively weak and compromised. Sometimes the challenge has been compounded by the limited pool of qualified reviewers for some fields of study. In some situations, the challenge has been compounded by the need to mitigate potential conflict of interest, especially in academic and professional fields that are new or that are not offered by many institutions. Sometimes some reviewers have been involved in successive assessment on the pretext that there are few equally qualified experts. A related challenge has been to mitigate the potential bias arising from past and concurrent institutional affiliations of reviewers or even that of the secretariat charged with managing the peer review process.

Perceptions of peer review process

Peer review is expected to generate candid reviews and evaluations of institutions and their programmes unaffected by personal feelings or institutional affiliation and personal biases of the peer reviewers. Yet, there have been varied reactions and perceptions to peer reviews such that the process itself has been singled out as problematic for the realization of quality and excellence. The identification of reviewers, their orientation and conduct have been subject to misrepresentation.

The screening process, where it has been followed religiously has resulted in weaning out those who do not have the required qualifications or who are conflicted or lack significant experience attained after earning the minimum academic or professional qualification. The challenge has been in administrative area. Until recently, appointment to administrative roles and position of college and university registrar did not require postgraduate qualification and indeed until recently even public higher education institutions did not prioritize postgraduate training of registrars to doctoral level.

Some higher education institutions have been resisting the peer review process on account of lack of trust, for instance, integrity of peer reviewers drawn from higher education institutions perceived to be competitors. Hence, pondering on the effectiveness of peer review, it is important to reflect on the need to change organisational cultures- the assumptions, beliefs, values and behaviours of higher education managers towards quality but also collaboration and partnership. The challenge of working in silos affects both the old and new, public and private higher education institutions, and among private institutions, both church and non-church affiliated higher education institutions.

Where peer review selection has not taken full account of declared and undeclared institutional affiliations or potential conflict of interest, leadership of institutions being assessed has objected to the involvement of peer experts whom they consider to be conflicted. Instances of conflict would include being a student in a postgraduate programme of a university or being a former employee of an institution regardless of the circumstance surrounding the exit from that employment. Most of those that have been identified as conflicted have voluntarily or involuntarily withdrawn from the process upon the insistence of the institutions concerned, notwithstanding assurances from the peer review team members that they would be objective.

Sometimes resistance to peer review surfaces at the end of the process and it is mounted to contest potential unfavourable assessment results and often the focus has been on perceived shortfalls in the quality of the assessment, and sometimes on account of unsubstantiated allegations such as standards used or expectations being in conflict with the religious values and ethos of an institution. Some institutions have resented the quality of feedback especially where it is explicit and could easily lead to identification of persons within the institution who might have shared adverse information to the disadvantage the institution.

A point to emphasise is that contrary to expectations and despite best efforts to demystify the processes, peer review is shrouded in mystery. Within higher education institutions there is an element of suspicion fuelled by the fear of the unknown. Allegations of real or imagined bias or unfair practice or collusion or corruption are rife. Some allegations suggest that some institutions pay their way to registration or accreditation, that some review teams collect money, which works to the disadvantage of those institutions that do not. Yet, when advised to substantiate the allegations or to provide details and even advised to report allegations to relevant prosecutorial authorities, the next step has been withdrawal of the allegation. It appears some unsubstantiated allegations are a tacit mechanism for obtaining sympathy and favourable consideration.

Peer review calls for certain degree of honesty that some institutions are not ready to open up to. In a classic case relating to biased recruitment of relatives, reviewers were discredited apparently for raising questions about the competences of a member of teaching staff who was a close relation to the head of the institution. Yet, the accreditation of another institution, which had employed administrative and teaching staff who had completed undergraduate training in another institution that had failed an assessment for re-accreditation fuelled perceptions that the whole peer review process was either unreliable or perhaps compromised.

Enhancing the quality of peer review process

Enhancing the quality of peer review will require addressing gaps in information and minimizing the risk of bias. Apparently, selection of peer reviewers works to the advantage of long serving experts, those with high social capital, and a 'big' name. Those who are well networked and known stand a better chance of being invited to participate as peer reviewers. New and upcoming experts may not have the same opportunity to grow as a result of the crowding out effect. It takes a while for new experts to get accepted and enjoy the same status as old timers. Hence, new reviewers are likely to be rejected or ignored because they are unknown and untested by those responsible for decision making. It is important to note that some may be rejected for undisclosed reasons and yet others for perceived conflict of interest as highlighted already. Those that are eventually accepted, have to demonstrate their worthiness. One way is to be proactive, objective and being timely in submission of reports. Yet, a fundamental question has been to understand whether the objectivity of the process changes from team to team or person to person. Is it possible that review results may change by changing reviewers?

To enhance the quality of the peer review process there is a need for serious rethinking of the conduct of assessments, perhaps starting from the selection of experts, their orientation and training, to the monitoring and evaluation of their performance. Effective results require that there is commitment to apply standards and criteria diligently to enhance both quality improvement and accountability. Peer reviewers have to be constructive, honest, and polite in the line of work. A standard requirement for declaring conflicts of interest should be adhered to and this must be done early enough to safeguard the integrity of the process. In view of the nature of higher education, those who serve as reviewers must be fully acquainted with the nature of the institutions they are assigned to evaluate. They need to respect the identity and integrity of the institutions or their programmes. This principle does not stop peer reviewers from examining, critiquing and offering advice; rather it pushes institutions to take control over the quality assurance of their programme offerings and safeguard academic autonomy. The complementarity between external and internal review processes is thereby enhanced. The importance of external quality assurance is enhanced through proper selection of peer reviewers and effective handling and managing of conflicts of interest as stated above. Consistence, effective use of standardized quality tools; training emphasizing the importance of focusing on issues under review and evidence availed, evidence based decisions informed by facts or the use of reliable information cannot be overemphasized. Involvement of foreign expertise, where is it feasible, provides another layer of external validation and should be used where necessary.

Sometimes a major point of contention has been the competence of reviewers, which is perceived from a combination of factors that include academic and professional training or qualifications, experience as teachers, researchers, examiners and administrators, and institutional politics. While some of the challenges in capacity can be addressed through orientation and trainings of different duration, others have a lingering and malignant effect on stakeholder perceptions. Nevertheless, it is pertinent that those who accept to be peer reviewers should endeavour to contribute to the attainment of desirable quality results. It is pertinent that the process is well governed by ensuring that standards, tools and scoring criteria are applied diligently focusing on quality improvements and ensuring the accountability of institutions. The reviewers should be constructive and honest. Those who are conflicted should declare conflicts of interest and voluntarily recuse themselves from participating in the processes. It is also pertinent that reviewers are dedicated and demonstrate their commitment to the promotion and pursuit of academic integrity. They need to show respect towards institutions being assessed. Respect in this regard goes beyond relationships between scholars as peers to respect of the academic autonomy, the identity and integrity of institutions or programmes being assessed

Conclusion

This chapter has emphasised the character and importance of the peer review process as used in quality assurance of institutions and programmes. Given that most of the peer reviewers are drawn from the higher education sector the peer review process is a form of control modelled on the concept of the evaluative state, a concept which became relevant and usefully applied in the 1980s in Western Europe. The attributes of an evaluative state include the understanding that deregulation has to be promoted by the state through mechanisms that make regulation possible through quasi-state bodies, which in effect imply devolved systems akin to self-regulation. Self-regulation becomes an important means of making institutions responsible. Effective self-regulation of higher education, however, requires pre-defined procedures and responsive structures supporting teaching, research and community service. To that extent, peer review becomes a "more subtle and sophisticated system of state surveillance" (Jongbloed 2007). As a practice, peer review can be perceived squarely as a form of community service geared to the advancement of scholarship, good management and governance of higher education and the pursuit of excellence. Excellence in this sense would include the performance of ordinary tasks extraordinarily well, absence of bias and deceit, willingness to acceptance results and commitment to continuous improvement by the regulated.

Chapter 6

Quality Rating of Higher Education in Malawi

Introduction

Provision of quality and relevant education is a governance and management issue. For this reason, governments around the world have legislated quality assurance. The United Nations 2030 Agenda (Sustainable Development Goals- SDGs) and African Union's Agenda 2063 known as the "Africa we Want" have emphasized the need for quality and relevant education at all levels. It is understood that achieving quality goes beyond improving upon what happens in the lecture theatre and laboratories to consideration of the enduring impact higher education has on employability of graduates, economic competitiveness, prosperity of nations and socio-cultural transformation of society. The African Union's Agenda 2063 place emphasis on economic and political integration of the continent, hence integrating the pursuit for quality education and political goals of a united continent. Quality assurance, even where it is perceived as a national sovereignty issue, it is in fact much bigger and better pursued and achieved through collaboration, benchmarking and peer learning. It means higher education institutions should perceive and pursue quality as a means of securing their place regionally, at continental and perhaps global level. The key challenge has been inconsistent standards and practices across institutions and education jurisdictions; making harmonization of quality assurance processes a topical issue.

Sustainable Development Goals (SGDs), especially goal number 4, advocates for access, equity, inclusiveness and life-long learning opportunities for all (United Nations).[36] The challenge with massification is that in the absence of complementary investment in infrastructure, equipment and personnel is recipe for serious compromise of quality. The false dilemma is the perception that

---

[36] United Nations, Transforming Our World: The 2030 Agenda for Sustainable Development.
https://sustainabledevelopment.un.org/content/documents/21252030%20Agenda%20for%20Sustainable%20Development%20web.pdf

increasing access should ordinarily lead to less concentration of effort, less commitment to maintenance of good standards, and less focus on academic rigour in admission and assessment practices. That understanding implies good quality education means standards that a privileged few only can afford and sustain. Such is an elitist view of quality as it implies the masses cannot be satisfied at the same level of quality as the elite would. In the spirit of liberalization, which promulgates the opening up of higher education provision to the masses through public, private and for profit providers, massification responds to rising demand and the means include diversification of modes of admission of learners, delivery of content and greater use of technologies of mass broadcasting and open, distance and e-learning approaches. The quality turn alluded to seeks to popularize the pursuit of quality in the framework of liberalization and massification. It is a call for greater accountability by stakeholders from proprietors, be they public and state or private, the students, bodies funding higher education or consuming its output, including the industry.

It follows that institutionalization of quality assurance practices, policies and regulations are necessary to be pursued and advocated for aggressively by all key stakeholders. Critical to this discussion is the need to establish, institutionalize and embed a quality culture, good practices, and provide clear sense of direction understood by all key stakeholders. Consensus is required to set up and consolidate an organizational culture appropriate for achieving quality higher education by addressing specific challenges such as:

a) human resource gaps- the shortage of well trained staff;
b) under resourcing of teaching and learning, underequipping of libraries, learning resources centres, studios and laboratories;
c) perennial budget deficits;
d) ineffective quality control measures; dysfunctional performance management systems, monitoring and evaluation systems; and
e) inadequate contextualization of the curricula and programmes to national priorities.

Addressing the issues stated above is necessary as it will ensure that learning is taking place in premises that are both purpose built and fit for purpose. Students will be taught by well qualified staff and to the best of the instructors' abilities. Further, there will be appropriate match between requirements and available resources. It is also necessary that higher education institutions should have systems that ensure that students are assessed and graded fairly. These conditions cannot be achieved if some higher education institutions continue engaging staff who do not meet the minimum academic qualifications and skills requirements.

Liberalization of higher education read as opening up and commercialization of higher education has resulted in drastic expansion of enrolment in higher education despite significant decrease in public expenditure on higher education per capita. The quality turn means that private providers should be equally pro-quality as much as they are pro-profit. According to Grant Harman specific areas of concern in this quality debate should be how to maintain standards, how to benchmark processes and practices to either national or international norms, how to maintain and improve teaching and learning, and how to provide sufficient financial and other resources to achieve and advance quality. The new turn places premium on achieving quality outcomes; the establishment and maintenance of appropriate internal management processes to monitor achievement, ensure high achievement standards and improvements in quality; and how to convince major stakeholders that systems and competent and ensuring quality outputs (Harman 1996). It follows, as Harman noted, management processes and assessment of outputs should also focus on the needs of the stakeholders and the labour market at large. That is, education and training should not be devoid of relevant industry and society sensitive reference points. This chapter delves into quality rating of higher education, understood as a measure of the quality and effectiveness of institutional provisions.

Quality assurance in higher education

Quality assurance has been conceptualized as a systematic and objective evaluation of how higher education institutions are operating as part of a process of enhancing the pursuit and achievement of academic excellence. Quality, however, means a level of performance and it is therefore a measure of reliability, consistency as well as fitness for purpose, fitness of purpose, and conformance to specifications and capability to meeting objectives, stakeholders' needs and requirements. Quality assurance serves the purpose of building stakeholder confidence ensuring that the quality provisions (inputs, processes and outcomes) fulfil expectations or measure up to threshold minimum requirements.[37] Quality enhancement conveys a different reality, that of planned activities and steps to bring about continuous improvement, achieve effectiveness and efficiency to each specific situation of higher education, in terms of the learning experiences and students outcomes.[38] These understandings represent a new turn to the discourse quality and academic excellence. According to Grant Harman in the past quality concerns in universities and government agencies were stated in terms such as academic standards, standards of degrees and diplomas, credibility of student assessment, and accountability. Specific areas of concerns were how to maintain academic standards and benchmarking processes to national or international norms, how to maintain and improve levels of teaching and learning, and how to provide sufficient financial and other resources to achieve quality higher education. The new turn places premium on achieving quality outcomes; the establishment of appropriate internal management processes to monitor achievement, and ensuring high achievement standards and improvements; and how to convince or assure major stakeholders that institutions and systems are doing a competent job of ensuring quality outputs (Harman 1996). While the old focus was concerned greatly about inputs and national and international academic standards, the new turn is much more concerned with management processes, assessment of output, and how well the output meets employer's needs.[39] Therefore, matters of quality are intertwined with market relevance to the same degree governance is part of this debate.

The quality rating used to date in Malawi is the accreditation and evaluation framework. The components of this framework include

---

[37] http://www.qualityresearchinternational.com/glossary/

[38] A statement derived from the website of Macau University of Science and Technology, https://www.must.edu.mo/en/qa/qaintro

[39] Grant Harman (1996) Quality Assurance for Higher Education: Developing and Managing Quality Assurance for Higher Education Systems and Institutions in Asia and The Pacific, Asia-Pacific Centre of Educational Innovation for Development (ACEID) Bangkok.

http://unesdoc.unesco.org/images/0010/001040/104046E.pdf

the minimum standards for higher education, assessment tools and a rating system. Developed in the 2014 – 15 period, the standards specify the requirements for governance, infrastructure, policies, programmes and resources and management processes. Peer or expert reviewers[40] drawn from the higher education sector and industry identified on the basis of their qualifications and experience support assessment of institutions and programme. The assessment tools operationalize provisions in the minimum standards and serve as objective guide in the quality review process. To ensure objectivity and in recognition of the primary role of institutions in the provision of quality education, institutions are required to prepare self-assessment reports using the same tools that are used by external peer reviewers and the results of the self-assessment and peer review process are supposed to be examined to inform decisions.

The indicators used are objective though reviewers make subjective judgments when awarding scores. Objective indicators are not dependent on the person doing the counting (Clarke 2002). For example, if two people were tasked to compute the student–faculty ratio or assess book collection and reading space in a library of a particular institution, they should come up with the same result (given the same formula and zero computational errors). Likewise, if peer reviewers were asked to locate the policy or appraise the application of the admission criteria in terms of adherence to minimum standards, the outcome should be objective in a number of areas, though there are likely to be subjective aspects when it comes to scoring. Subjectivity can be minimized by proper orientation of reviewers, reviewers working in teams, cross checking and vetting the scoring, asking reviewers to provide evidence for scores awarded, among other measures that can ensure standardized result.

Quality rating of higher education institutions

A gold standard for measuring quality of higher education is quality of the graduate, that is, the knowledge, skills and

---

[40] As presented in the previous chapter, a typical reviewer will have a master level qualification, several years of professional experience as a lecturer or administrator, industrial experience and for academic reviewers of the rank of senior lecturer or equivalent.

competences that graduates acquire and can demonstrate. Therefore, an important milestone in higher education is the shift from learning objectives to learning outcomes. Learning objectives manifest autocratic posture to learning emphasizing what the learner should learn while the learning outcomes are result oriented, focusing on the abilities and benefits individuals and society can realize as a result of education and training. Yet, in the course of learning and even thereafter, learning continues to be represented by success in examinations, examinations grades, credits earned and accumulated and qualifications received. The proliferation and diversity of higher education institutions imply that comparisons between graduates from different education systems and institutions remain a daunting challenge, and even more challenging is the gap of tallying training received and graduate competences, understood as what a learner should know, understand and be able to do. Ordinarily, lower level qualifications should represent attainment of basic, generic and/or vocational skills. Holders of basic and generic qualifications should ordinarily work effectively under supervision. The middle level qualifications are appropriate for entry into professional positions that require workers who can perform independently. Finally, higher level qualifications should emphasize capacity to analyse, synthesize, evaluate and innovate, create new knowledge and may also include ability to lead and manage people and processes. Consequently, from a quality rating point of view the challenge for curriculum developers is one of designing curricula and ensuring appropriate mix, pacing and gradation of learning activities and outcomes

In practice, institutional and programme accreditation have become important ways of validating quality. Initially over a period of two years, between 2016 and 2018 and then thereafter the National Council for Higher Education (NCHE) has conducted assessments for accreditation of higher education institutions in Malawi using a quality rating process modelled on the African Quality Rating Mechanism (AQRM). AQRM is an instrument devised by the African Union Commission, which aims to provide an objective measure of quality of African higher education institutions through institutional self-assessment. Another key feature is that the quality rating process conforms to the statutory provisions for both institutional and programme accreditation. It draws on good practices in Africa (Kenya, Lesotho, Namibia,

Nigeria, South Africa, Tanzania, and Uganda), European Higher Education Area and some accreditation bodies in the United States of America, for example, the Southern Association of Colleges and Schools, Commission on Colleges.

In terms of its design and application, AQRM includes criteria against which institutions can assess their own quality levels and therefore assist institutions to benchmark progress in quality development in every area of education provision and research. As Ayewole (2010) put it, AQRM is not a ranking instrument and as such may not be used to promote the listing of institutions in a league table. Instead, it is a tool to help institutions rate themselves on some quality criteria and to recognize the excellence residing within them. Developed through a process involving desk-top review of the Worldwide Web and a wide range of academic databases to identifying key best practices in the field and to determine the current trends and initiatives in Africa, the accreditation and evaluation framework is anchored by the minimum standards, database of reviewers, and tools that customize the minimum standards to an assessment regime. A rating system devised on a scale of 0 – 4 is used through out to rank areas of assessment, both in an internal self-assessment and external assessment. The rating mechanism allows for the classification of higher education institutions and programmes into quality based categories: 'unsatisfactory quality; 'satisfactory quality'; and 'excellent quality'. In terms of actual rating scores or rating of 0 – 1.99 represent unsatisfactory performance while 2 – 2.99 represent satisfactory performance and 3 – 4 represent excellent performance. Using such a rating on six parameters of infrastructure, library, e-Learning resources, management of infrastructure, governance and finances, higher education institutions may be rated for quality or accredited for excellent rating, accredited with conditions for satisfactory rating and not accredited for unsatisfactory rating. The rating of institutions is done prior to the rating of the programmes. Ordinarily, once an institution is deemed to be unsatisfactory (that it is not of acceptable level of quality), the programmes even if they are well developed the rating may unlikely be satisfactory given the interdependences between institutional and programme assessments. However, an unsatisfactory rating for an institution may not stop an assessment of the programmes.

The results may show areas of strength and weakness, or where each institution had been performing well or not. Consequently, institutions are made aware of their performance rating and thus empowered to enhance performance in the areas of their strength, and by taking remedial measures, also to improve areas where they were found to be underperforming or lagging. Continuous improvement is therefore possible.

The ratings, where objectively conducted, would provide objective and perhaps indisputable measure of quality of the higher education institutions per parameter. While the ratings can be used to compare institutions per parameter, the overall rating aggregate may be a good yardstick for ranking the institutions concerned. Given that the overall rating may not be a useful measure for ranking purposes, this serves to underscore the need for understanding that the value of the rating, if it is ever to be used, should be to support institutions to focus on what needs to be improved in their programming. Another aspect is that although the ratings signify meaningful differences in quality, there is no differentiation between institutions within the same rating category, save where there are significant differences in the corresponding qualitative recommendations. However, there is significant difference between institutions in different categories and the differences in the rating have reputational effects on the state of quality of the institutions but also their programmes. The ratings are an invitation to all stakeholders to engage in meaningful discussions on the quality of education offered and how best to enhance areas of strength in the interest of continuous improvement (African Union Commission 2018).

The operation of the ratings show unequivocally that public higher education institutions provide satisfactory to excellence learning facilities, e-learning resources and management of infrastructure. Unsatisfactory ratings were noted for some public institutions in the areas of library services, governance and management of finances. The unsatisfactory ratings along these three parameters were however observed at the satellite centres/campuses, which by their designation are not fully fledged institutions. Generally, private higher education institutions affiliated to church bodies perform relatively well than other private higher education institutions. Most church affiliated universities and colleges tend to operate in own facilities and there is a demonstrated commitment towards investment in infrastructure, including library facilities. Most church affiliated universities and colleges happened to be one of the many social investments and commitments. Operating a private higher education institution is perceived as a commitment to works of charity rather than a profit making venture.

Apparently, the state and adequacy of infrastructure and the effectiveness of the management of infrastructure and the systems and processes reflect the commitment of proprietors and management of each institution to quality education. Institutions with good infrastructure invest an equal measure of quality in the programmes support and staff training in order to derive maximum value from the investment in infrastructure. The costs of developing and maintaining infrastructure tend to be higher than other costs combined save for remuneration. Hence, institutions that have quality infrastructure oftentimes tend to score better in other areas as well. This explains the higher than average scores registered not just for public higher education institutions but also institutions established by church affiliated institutions, especially those that have a long history in the provision of education and are also well known for running schools that provide quality primary and secondary education, teacher training for primary schools and nursing education. The long history of investment in social services suggests that in the long term non-church or unaffiliated higher education institutions may eventually begin to invest more and effectively in physical infrastructure, equipment and system improvements subject to instituting effective progressive support systems. In other words, being for profit and pro-quality should not be perceived as mutually exclusive endevours.

In general terms, some private universities and colleges do not fare well in two areas of library resources and finances. Most obtained satisfactory scores in the areas of e-learning resources, management of infrastructure and governance. This demonstrates the importance of e-learning resources in the absence of investment in books and physical libraries, which are generally considered expensive from the point of cost and rather out dated from the point of view of the rapid changes in knowledge and technology. Related challenges have been lack of relevance and datedness of collections. This challenge was articulated earlier by Francis

Nyamnjoh writing about the resilience of colonial education in Africa in the following words:

> Most African university libraries are underfunded, struggle to keep pace with the latest publications of relevance, and are often desperately under stocked and at the mercy of donors dying to dump old and outdated publications as a sort of intellectual 'toxic' waste. Libraries that are well stocked even with material of direct relevance to critical scholarship informed by African perspectives and predicaments may find such books and journals under-consulted because of curricula and scholarly traditions that pay scant attention to African sources (Nyamnjoh, 2012:141).

In this regard Nyamnjoh draws attention to the need to strike a balance between availability and utility of library resources. Lack of contextualization of the curricula is a challenge that is beyond libraries and library executives. More concerted effort will be required from technical, policy and financing perspectives to dismantle the resilience of obsolete curricula.

The satisfactory rating on the management of infrastructure registered by many institutions (both public and private) reflects the commitment that institutions make in their preparation for external assessment. In many cases old buildings are painted, floors and furniture refurbished and broken windowpanes and ceiling fixed. A satisfactory rating on governance is a plus on most newly established private universities, which have embraced governance structures propagated by the state to ensure that institutions do not fail as a result of poor and dysfunctional governance systems. This provision is in keeping with the third pillar for higher education, that of governance and management, which is a call for proprietors and governors of higher education institutions to work towards institutionalization of effective, open, transparent and accountable governance systems and processes. There is still room for improvement as it appears that in some cases there is still need for radical transformation, especially in some church affiliated higher education institutions where the clergy have moved in to replace non-clerical leadership soon after institutions gained accreditation, sometimes on the pretext of curbing mismanagement and falling staff morale.

Further, the results demonstrated the practical importance of self-assessment. Institutions that conducted honest self-assessment earlier had the advantage of knowing areas for improvement and they proceeded to align their budget commitments to address shortfalls. This is the benefit of self-awareness, whose value and benefit is correlated to the drive for self-improvement. Where there is a commitment for continuous improvement, over time and eventually that commitment translate to a culture of quality. Therefore, it can be argued that quality rating supports the development of institutional level quality assurance practices that organically inform the development of internal quality standards, process and procedures. Several institutions have moved to galvanize their quality assurance regimes by institutionalizing quality assurance units with reporting arrangements that emphasize that the institutions are eventually taking quality as a priority thereby according quality assurance the attention it deserves.

Enhancing the quality rating of higher education institutions

This analysis provided above drew on seven public institutions and 18 private institutions that were assessed using internationally benchmarked assessment criteria, the Accreditation and Evaluation Framework, which was modelled on the African Quality Rating Mechanism (AQRM). The analysis focused on assessing the institution. The other side is programme assessment, which was not covered. Therefore, the accreditation results presented above provide a general guide on the overall quality of the institutions concerned. Institutions with an overall rating of 2.0 or higher provide satisfactory teaching and learning environments in comparison to those with ratings of less than 2.0. Most public institutions appear to provide satisfactory to good learning environments. Apparently, public institutions command necessary resources both material and nonmaterial, support from internal and external stakeholders, which are critical to ensuring further quality improvements. Yet, there is room for further improvement bearing in mind the systemic challenges that public higher education institutions experience.

The results do not provide a ranking system much as they provide insight into the quality of the environment in which teaching and learning takes place and the prevailing governance and management systems. If they are to be used for ranking purpose, certainly the ranking will be less about the quality of graduates from the institutions and relevance of the training, which may require an insight into the ratings of the programmes, staff complement, admission processes and assessment ratings, benchmarking, research output and rating on the extent of internationalization of the programmes. Suffice to state that the results demonstrate the responsiveness of institutions to government policy on higher education. First government has made a commitment to expand access to higher education and the liberalization of the sector measured by the number of private institutions is yielding result. The rise of private higher educations is a window of opportunity for increasing space and diversifying programme offerings. Private universities have been observed to be more responsive to emerging needs in human resource development than public universities whose response rate and pace of change is often grounded by bureaucratic red tape. The challenge, however, is ensuring that increasing access and diversity of programme offerings do not lead to serious deficiency in the quality of education being provided. It follows that the pursuit of increasing access and ensuring that there is equity should not be at the expense of quality. There is need to balance access with quality and at the same time ensure that the higher education being offered is relevant and responsive to industry and societal needs. A robust system for registering and accrediting institutions is needed and for greater efficiency should be enhanced and complemented by rigorous on-going process of programme reviews at institutional level and regular monitoring and audits at the regulatory agency level. Higher education institutions which have the primary responsibility of ensuring quality higher education must be empowered and provided clear guidelines on how to develop and review programmes using tested and well benchmarked models of programme design and review. Regular monitoring and evaluation, and institutional and programme audits, should become a norm and therefore an integral part of internal quality control within higher education institutions. Such measures will mitigate the risks of non-compliance with threshold standards and associated risks to quality.

Quality rating of institutions and programme should counter the growing threat of credentialism. Drawing on a variety of sources, Garwe (2015) suggested that credentialism is an ideology of social selection in which academic qualifications are perceived as providing measurable and sufficient indicators of a person's expertise, aptitudes or attributes necessary to perform tasks, to give status or occupy élite positions. For Johnson (2006), however, credentialism feeds the urge for fake qualifications and hence the relationship is more direct as captured in the following phraseology: "the employer pretends to need a degree; the employee pretends to have one." The real challenge is that credentialism and aspiration for status and privileges associated with various higher education qualifications, especially doctorates, feed the curiosity associated with fake qualifications, but also the tendency among university and college students to plagiarise and those without access to seek and use honorary qualifications injudiciously. In some situations, growing credentialism has made individuals seek and earn a living from selling or facilitating acquisition of fake and honorary degrees. Some obtain honorary degrees from little known institutions and therefore the value and level of prestige to be gained is as insignificant as the paper itself. The challenge to date is that some fake and honorary qualifications from alleged western universities have been used to secure teaching positions in higher education institutions in some developing countries. The implications on quality of teaching and research have been catastrophic. Writing for India, Sanjay Srivasatava (2015) offered an important lesson on academic quality and rigour with a particular focus on the quality of university teachers, while noting the challenge posed by inbreeding and articulation of underprepared doctoral candidates into the university system as teachers and researcher. He observed that:

> "One of the key reasons for the appalling state of the university system is that a vast number of university teachers utilise their position to perpetuate patron-client relationships rather than participate in or encourage serious and rigorous research. Hence, each year around the country, thousands of MPhils and PhDs are supervised and – mysteriously – passed by examiners. All along the line it creates a network of patrons and clients who scratch each other's backs. The effect of this is a mass of doctorate-holding individuals who find employment within the university system and who – in turn –

perpetuate the same educational standards they have experienced. It is an endless cycle" (Srivasatava 2015)[41].

It is pertinent that all higher education institutions should strengthen their quality assurance systems as well enhance their research and publication agenda by providing more resources, including capacity for enhanced screening of qualifications presented by those seeking tenured, adjunct and other academic positions. Further, universities should introduce a rating system that will eventually categorize scholars in terms of their capacity as scholars and for each category and in recognition of needs particular to each set of scholars, provide capacity enhancing incentives and reward system other than those available and often used for promotion purposes. Both staff and students should be capacitated to understand the importance of quality research and ethics.

---

[41] Online source: https://thewire.in/education/fake-degrees-is-not-the-problem-obsession-with-degrees-is

Chapter 7

Setting and Operating Quality Assurance Units in Higher Education Institutions

Introduction

Legitimate higher education institutions strive to meet and ensure that their business processes comply with threshold standards for academic excellence, that is, best practices in teaching, research and outreach. This expectation applies to all processes including planning and budgeting, recruitment of staff, admission of students, teaching, assessment and supervision, and certifying of learning and achievement. Hence, the leadership and proprietors of higher education institutions ought to strategically reflect on how to manage everyday processes that have such a bearing on quality. Higher education institutions that aspire to be world class centres of academic excellence cannot miss the pursuit for excellence across all areas. The meaning of excellence, how it may be realised and whether it can be achieved has been a subject of scholarly interest.

Renowned physicist Albert Einstein, for instance, observed that "Excellence is doing a common thing in an uncommon way".[42] Einstein's proposition is therefore a challenge to higher education institutions to be quality minded in every aspect. It requires a level of creativity and innovation to be excellent in small things. This is pertinent considering that higher education is big business and excellence may not happen by chance. Aristotle, also a prominent figure in Greek history and philosophy, viewed excellence as an art: "Excellence is an art won by training and habituation. We do no act rightly because we have virtue or excellence but we rather have those because we have acted rightly. We are what we repeatedly do. Excellence, then, is not an act but a habit".[43] The key to cultivating habits that may catalyse academic excellence is in Plato's view borne

---

[42] Some sources have attributed the same statement to Booker T. Washington, an African-American educator.

https://www.brainyquote.com/quotes/booker_t_washington_382201

[43] https://www.forbes.com/quotes/659/#:~:text=Excellence%20is%20an%20art%20won%20by%20training%20and%20habituation.,an%20act%20but%20a%20habit An alternative source is https://wist.info/aristotle/1334/

in practice. Plato, the author of The Republic argued that "Excellence is not a gift, but a skill that takes practice. We do not act "rightly' because we are "excellent". In fact, we achieve "Excellence" by acting rightly" [44]

The challenge to date is that liberalization, also read commercialization of higher education has resulted in drastic expansion of access, significant decrease in public expenditure on higher education, a rise in the number of private providers, some of which are callously profit oriented.[45] The key concern is how to assure and enhance quality? Grant Harman observed that in the past quality concerns in universities and government agencies took the form of terms such as academic standards, standards of degrees and diplomas, credibility of student assessment, and accountability. Specific areas of concern in that quality debate were how to maintain standards and benchmark the processes to national or international norms, how to maintain and improve levels of teaching and learning, and how to provide sufficient financial and other resources to achieve the expected quality higher education. The new turn places premium on achieving quality outcomes; the establishment of appropriate internal management processes to monitor achievement, and ensuring high achievement standards and improvements in quality; and how to convince or assure major stakeholders that institutions and systems are doing enough in ensuring quality outputs (Harman 1996). While in the past focus was about inputs and national and international academic standards, the new turn is much more concerned with improving and enhancing management processes, assessment of output, and how well outputs meet employer and other needs.[46] Therefore, matters of quality are intertwined with matters of market relevance and quality as a governance issue. Critical to the quality discourse is the need to establish a culture of quality, whereby everyone within an

---

[44] https://www.goodreads.com/quotes/106625-excellence-is-not-a-gift-but-a-skill-that-takes

[45] Masanja, V. G. and S. Lwakabamba., 'Liberalization of higher education in Sub-Saharan Africa', RUFORUM Working Document Series (ISSN 1607-9345) No. 14 (2): 1-7 Available from *http://repository.ruforum.org*

[46] Grant Harman (1996) Quality Assurance for Higher Education: Developing and Managing Quality Assurance for Higher Education Systems and Institutions in Asia and The Pacific, Asia-Pacific Centre of Educational Innovation for Development (ACEID) Bangkok.
http://unesdoc.unesco.org/images/0010/001040/104046E.pdf

institution is aware of and follow quality guidelines consistently, everyone is committed to taking quality-focused actions, everyone hears others talking and pursuing quality, and feels quality all around them.

This chapter looks into how higher education institutions around the world are pursuing excellence by establishing quality assurance units. To this extent it seeks to contribute to the discourse on quality assurance and enhancement in an era characterized by twin processes of liberalization and massification, where liberalization relates to the opening up of higher education provision to private and for profit providers while massification is a response to rising demand for higher education and through the diversification of modes of delivery, greater use of technologies of mass broadcasting and open, distance and e-learning approaches. Institutionalization of quality assurance best practices, policies and regulations are therefore reflected upon as necessary, and advocated for aggressively as many higher education institutions around the globe have come to realize. It is based on case studies drawn from four continents. It is an attempt to identify best practices and promote proper alignment of mandates, functions and structures. The purpose will be to open a discussion on how to set up and institutionalize quality assurance (QA) units as a means to harnessing the quality culture. The case studies presented in this chapter have not been selected for their completeness and representativeness. The key challenge to be noted from the use of such resources is lack of uniformity and comparability of information. For some entities, detailed information was available in the national languages and the challenge imposed by language barriers cannot be underestimated.

Global trends and mandate

Setting up a quality assurance unit is an innovative and emerging practice in higher education regulation in the 21st Century. It is premised in the recognition that higher education institutions bear the primary responsibility for the quality of their services. Hence setting up the unit is a demonstration of institutional commitment to quality and excellence. Many higher education institutions around the world have or are in the process of setting up quality assurance units[47]. Like external quality assurance, the factors that have made it necessary and an area of interest in higher education regulation include globalisation, massification and internationalization of higher education; liberalisation associated with the entry of private players; growing private expenditure on higher education in form of tuition and other fees in both public and private higher education institutions; alliances between institutions and across border provision of education; the proliferation of new modes of delivery that include open, distance and e-learning approaches; and the growing diversity of students entering higher education and diversity of their needs which call for innovative and deliberate and systematic regulation. It follows that the discourse on quality assurance units cannot be isolated from trends that have inspired practices such as the establishment of national higher education regulatory bodies, national qualifications frameworks (NQF) and the emergence of higher education areas.[48] As the increase in tertiary education provision, particularly by private providers, and the movement of people and educational institutions across national borders have led to growing demand for quality assurance mechanisms, national governments and international bodies have to use comparable standards by which to judge how institutions are responding to calls for harmonization of programmes and qualifications, to assure the quality of education and increase competitiveness and international recognition of credentials. Quality assurance units are intended to contribute to harmonization of quality within institutions (bringing about harmony in terms of programme management across departments, faculties, schools, institutes, colleges, campuses, etc.) and ensure proper alignment to trends at national and internal levels.

By definition quality assurance units are best understood as an office established to monitor, control and enhance the quality of administrative and educational performance, and to reinforce the quality culture in the higher education.[49] The notion of enforcement implies that QA units are intended to enforce and monitor the

---

[47] International Institute for Educational Planning
http://unesdoc.unesco.org/images/0026/002613/261356e.pdf
[48] The European Higher Education Area (EHEA) is an example. The African Union Commission also embarked on a process to create the African higher education area with common standards for quality assurance.
[49] https://www.ppu.edu/p/en/administrative-departments/quality-assurance

quality assurance arrangements, to maintain and elevate quality outcomes within the institutions. Therefore, QA units represent deliberate effort to institutionalize quality, inculcate a culture of quality and standardise or harmonise quality assurance practices.[50] The units are expected to improve the educational environment through use of appropriate tools and criteria of evaluation. In the era of internationalization and globalization of higher education, this should lead to achievement of satisfactory and comparable standards within institutions and nationally, enhancing regional and international competitiveness as well. The question is whose mandate is it to establish quality assurance units and how should they function?

A key point of reference of quality assurance units is to operationalize and institutionalize quality processes, practices and procedures. It is understood that besides opening up access to higher education and training, quality should be an important consideration as it has a bearing on the relevance and marketability of programmes. Both have impacts on the quality of training and educational experience of students.[51] Where the state retains the powers to regulate higher education centrally, quality assurance units may be set up by law, for instance in Greece's Aristotle University of Thessaloniki and University of Patras.[52] In some countries, however, quality assurance units are established by decree or circular and this is the case for the Internal Quality Assurance Unit at universities in Sri Lanka, for example, University of Peradeniya whose quality assurance unit was established in 2016 in accordance with guidelines issued by the University Grants Commission Circular 04/2015.[53] In some countries quality assurance units are set up by senate resolution and therefore function without the force of the law as in the first instance but as a conventional practice established in the traditions, that is, the self-governing role of the universities. This is the case in a number of

---

[50] https://www.ucl.ac.uk/medical-school/current-mbbs-students/quality-assurance-unit

[51] https://www.pdn.ac.lk/centers/iqau/intdu.php

[52] The QA Unit of University of Patras was set up according to the provisions of Articles 14 and 80 of Law 4009/11 (195'A) and paragraph 5 of Article 83 of Law 4485/2017 (114 A'), in order to support and coordinate the quality assurance procedures of the University of Patras. https://www.upatras.gr/en/modip

[53] University of Peradeniya (n.d.) 'Internal Quality Assurance Unit', https://www.pdn.ac.lk/centers/iqau/index.php

countries in Canada, across Africa, as well as some European universities. For example, Canadian Institute of Technology's Quality Assurance Unit was first established in the academic year 2012-2013 by means of decision no. 16, dated 22 May 2013, of the Academic Senate.[54] Since then the unit has been reorganized in order to better reflect the changes of the academic and institutional structures. Yet in other instances quality assurance units operate as a unit or just an office within other functions. For example, in the University of Lisboa, Portugal the functions are performed by an office known as The Quality Assurance and Assessment Office and in terms of its mandate the office monitors quality assurance activities that are related to the accreditation of the study programmes offered by the University, and it is expected to offer technical and administrative support to the Quality Assurance Board.[55] In terms of operationalization the case studies provided in the subsequent section suggest different facets on how to organize and operationalize such units. Most of the case studies provided below are drawn from Europe (5), Asia (5) and Africa (4). Two case studies have been derived from Canada and Oceania. Functionally, the quality assurance units operate within each institution's ethos.

Quality assurance units in selected European universities

Five case studies will be explored: Quality Assurance Unit in University College of London Medical School (United Kingdom) and Aristotle University of Thessalonik (Greece), Quality Assurance Office in University of Kent (United Kingdom), Unit for Quality Assurance in University of Vienna (Austria) and Internal Quality Assurance Office of Albania University (Albania).

In the University College of London Medical School, the role of the Quality Assurance Unit is to ensure that high standards and good practice within the teaching, learning and assessment processes for undergraduate medical programme are recognised and rewarded, and problems are rapidly identified and addressed. The unit serves internal and external functions, including internal monitoring, and these functions revolve around the development

---

[54] CIT Quality Assurance Unit, http://cit.edu.al/en/cit-quality-assurance-unit-cit-qau/

[55] University of Lisboa (n.d.) 'The Quality Assurance and Assessment Office', https://www.ulisboa.pt/en/info/quality-assurance-and-assessment-office-0

and dissemination of teaching standards and guidelines; collecting feedback via student evaluation questionnaires (SEQs); and collecting other student experience data via online reporting systems which may include documenting concerns from students, their experiences, expectations, etc. about teaching and learning, research and community involvement. External monitoring, however, entails ensuring that procedures are established and maintained to respond in a transparent manner to national, professional, legislative and regulatory requirements.[56] In Aristotle University of Thessalonik the Quality Assurance Unit was set up according to article 14 of statute Greek law nr 4009/2011), whose roles can be summarized as follows: development of policies, strategies and processes to improve the institution, improvement of the quality assurance system; coordination and support of the evaluation processes of units; and support of the processes for external evaluation and certification of the programmes of studies.[57] At the University of Kent, United Kingdom, the Quality Assurance Office is part of a Unit for the Enhancement of Learning and Teaching (UELT) and is responsible for:[58]

i) maintaining and enhancing the processes by which the University assures the quality and standards of its awards;

ii) servicing the University Learning and Teaching Board, Programme Approval Sub-Committee, the Working Group on Regulations and Conventions, the Academic Audit Committee and the Senate Academic Review Committee;

iii) providing an administrative liaison between the University and its validated partners who deliver programmes of study leading to a University award under collaborative arrangements, and;

iv) working closely with the Faculties Support Office and the Graduate School, thus ensuring that there is a concerted and collaborative approach to all aspects of

---

[56] https://www.ucl.ac.uk/medical-school/current-mbbs-students/quality-assurance-unit

[57] https://www.auth.gr/en/units/8184

[58] university of Kent (n.d.) 'Unit of the Enhancement of Learning & Teaching', https://www.kent.ac.uk/uelt/about/quality.html

quality assurance and enhancement within the University.

In the University of Vienna similar functions are performed by the Unit for Quality Assurance whose defined mandate is to supports the University in its endeavour to ensure a high level of quality in its teaching and research activities and programmes of study. The unit is expected by its functionality to contribute to the development of quality assurance system and the concomitant quality criteria, methods and instruments. Quality assurance practices and standards are expected to be in line with the on-going endeavour to adhere to international standards for promoting a culture of quality and strengthening the university's ability to be responsive and responsible for its own affairs. Therefore, the unit is expected to contribute to the self-governing processes and enhanced autonomy of the university whose quality mantra is:

> "Quality assurance is the responsibility of all units and members of the University in their respective areas of activity. It aims at achieving the highest quality in research and teaching [...] The associated quality culture is the backbone of the University of Vienna's quality assurance"[59]

For Albanian University, Albania the Internal Quality Assurance Office is mandated to provide guidance, advice and support for the design and implementation of internal procedures of quality assurance in accordance with internal guidelines. The functionality of the office is guided by the need to improve and maintain high level academic and administrative services through: structures that promote the creation of quality culture; regular reporting of recommendations to the University Senate on matters related to improving the quality in the teaching and non-teaching fields; provision of services related to ensuring and improving teaching and learning quality; review and consideration of new international trends and best practice in the context of Quality Assurance; ensuring implementation of the procedures laid down with regard to quality; facilitating dissemination within the university of quality

---

[59] This is according to University of Vienna 2025 Development Plan. University of Vienna (n.d.) 'Quality Assurance', http://www.qs.univie.ac.at/en/

related information; and review of guidelines related to quality.[60] In terms of specific tasks and targets the internal quality assurance offices serves to:

- contribute to the improvement of education and research, and the development of individualism of different study programs;
- assist in their full accountability before the public actors and their status as evaluators;
- establish credibility among the community sustaining that the university meets national and international standards of academic quality;
- support departments in implementing the standards established by relevant AU structures and in preparing documents to be submitted to the accreditation agencies;
- conduct assessments of each department within the university to promote the fact that strengths are sustainable and weaknesses should be corrected;
- support departments in the creation of their strategic plan;
- encourage departments to perform self-assessment, including assessment performed by students;
- improve the research, teaching and learning quality;
- support university faculties and centres through the creation and development of quality assured internal system;
- meet expectations of students and university employees; and
- meet satisfaction and expectations related to benefits from university services;

Quality assurance units in Asian countries

For Asia, case studies that have been selected include Internal Quality Assurance Unit (IQAU) of Uva Wellassa University and

---

[60] Albanian University (n.d.) 'Internal Quality Assurance Unit', http://albanianuniversity.edu.al/en/internal-quality-assurance-unit/

University of Paradeniya both from Sri Lanka, the Quality Assurance Unit (QAU) in Universiti Teknologi Brunei, Brunei and the Quality Assurance Office (QAO) in Macau University of Science and Technology, Macau.

Uva Wellassa University's Internal Quality Assurance Unit (IQAU) has the mandate to oversee quality of all new and existing degree programs, faculties and units.[61] IQUA ensures that the Uva Wellassa University operates in conformity with external standards such as the Sri Lankan Qualification Framework and bodies like the Quality Assurance and Accreditation Council (QAAC) of Sri Lanka. The internal QA processes include: degree programme and module approval; receiving and processing student feedback; peer observation of academic teaching; managing external examiners; and periodic review of modules and degree programmes. Besides the University wide unit, there are also faculty level QA activities that are administered by Faculty QA Cell headed by Deans of Faculty. Similarly, for University of Paradeniya, Sri Lanka, the establishment of the internal quality assurance unit was a direct result of government directive contained in the recommendation of the University Grants Commission (UGC) to facilitate the University's quality assurance activities and to coordinate them with the QAAC at the UGC. The QA unit's role is perceived as that of complementing the external quality assurance processes. Therefore, the significance of having an IQAU is that it complements external quality assurance procedures which take place only at intervals. The quality assurance unit is better placed to assuring quality as a continuous and on-going process where all academic, administrative and support staff working in an institution must take responsibility for building quality into their day-to-day routine activities. Hence, a QA unit is considered the cornerstone of QA whose major functions include:[62]

- enhancing the quality and relevance of teaching and learning and responding to global trends on quality education by preparing guidelines on QA for the University/Institution;

---

[61] Uva Wellassa University (n.d.) 'Internal Quality Assurance Unit' (IQAU) http://www.uwu.ac.lk/academic/units/iqau/ .
[62] University of Peradeniya (n.d.) Internal Quality Assurance Unit', https://www.pdn.ac.lk/centers/iqau/intdu.php

- guiding and assisting the programme offering entities i.e., departments, faculties and institutes of the university to define program objectives, program outcomes and graduate profiles and support sustainable quality enhancement;
- developing standards and benchmarks for various academic and administrative activities of the university;
- organizing workshops, seminars and appropriate training for capacity building and promoting QA culture at all levels of the university;
- facilitating the creation of outcome-based education and student-centred learning throughout the university using technology for a participatory teaching and learning process;
- reviewing existing procedures for further improvement of delivery of teaching and learning;
- providing support to the study program offering academic units to conduct the self-assessment, external peer review and implement QA process at program level; and
- implementing QA reviews/audit and follow-up actions.

In Universiti Teknologi Brunei the Quality Assurance Unit (QAU) was formed in November 2011 with the prime focus of administering quality systems governing all academic matters in the University. The activities of the unit are guided by the Quality Unit Steering Committee. In terms of the functionality of the quality assurance unit, the following are its areas of focus:[63]

- ensuring continuous enhancement of the quality of teaching and learning,
- reviewing existing programmes of study every five years which would include input from external stakeholders, teaching staff, graduates and students.
- conducting annual review of modules related to each programme of study which includes end of module evaluation by teaching staff and students.

---

[63] Universiti Teknologi Brunei (n.d.) 'The Quality Assurance Unit', http://www.utb.edu.bn/academics/the-quality-assurance-unit-qau/

- serving as the repository for all documentation related to Quality which includes minutes of meetings; reports of examiners; reports on programme reviews; reports on modules reviews; accreditation reports; quality procedures; teaching materials and examination chapters etc.
- serving as the examination office for the University responsible for the administration of the University's examination including setting dates for examination periods and examination boards, internal and external moderation of examination, printing of examination, distribution of examination results to students, processing "Extenuating Circumstances" and "Absence from Examination" forms, etc.

While at Macau University of Science and Technology the Quality Assurance Office (QAO) was established in 2009 and its mission statement is: 'To ensure the highest quality learning, teaching, curricula, research and administration in the university through the development, implementation and continuous improvement of quality, quality improvement and quality enhancement in the university, and to ensure that the highest quality systems and procedures to achieve these operate.'[64] The work of the Quality Assurance Office and quality assurance processes across the university are guided by the following principles:

- Quality assurance and enhancement are developmental and are part of the university's strategy for ensuring the highest quality learning, teaching, curricula, research and academic operations and standards of the university.
- Quality assurance and enhancement are collaborative and cooperative.
- Quality assurance and enhancement are empowering and involve all areas and of the university, parties and stakeholders.

---

[64] https://www.must.edu.mo/en/qa

- Quality assurance and enhancement are designed to meet internal and external approval, accreditation and recognition requirements.
- Quality assurance and enhancement are ongoing and part of the university's strategies for continuous improvement and excellence;
- Quality assurance and enhancement practices at all areas of the university are documented, monitored, reviewed and evaluated.
- Quality assurance and enhancement are designed to promote institutional and public confidence in the academic standards of the university.
- Quality assurance and enhancement are transparent, systematic, rigorous and equitable.
- Quality assurance and enhancement focus on input, processes, outcomes and impact.
- Quality assurance and enhancement is a supported and facilitated process in the university.

In view of the principles states above the main responsibility of the Quality Assurance Office (QAO) is to provide leadership, guidance and support for QA at all levels and to support the institutional and faculty accreditation processes and content. The specific responsibilities are framed as follows:

- to formulate strategies, policies, systems, procedures and practices for the university's academic quality assurance and enhancement
- to promote and implement quality-related strategic developments within sustainable quality assurance and enhancement frameworks and procedures and in accordance with the university vision and strategic planning;
- to promote the culture of academic quality within the university
- to develop policies and guidelines on teaching evaluation, programme review and student learning assessment

- to monitor, review, audit, evaluate and continuously develop the university's quality together with its quality assurance and enhancement strategies, frameworks and procedures at all levels of the university, for the promotion of academic excellence in learning, teaching and research;
- to provide administrative and substantive support for quality assurance and enhancement at all levels of the university, and to support the institutional and course accreditation processes and contents for external organizations and agencies;
- to monitor, review, audit, evaluate and continuously develop institutional and course accreditation;
- to advise on program and course approval and development;
- to oversee the allocation of teaching development grants and organize teaching enhancement activities; and
- to compile publications on learning and teaching enhancement.

The four case studies cited above from Asia suggests that quality units should focus on strengthening QA process at institutional level and serve to respond positively to standards and guidelines set by external quality assurance agencies.

Quality Assurance Units in African universities

For Africa case studies have been drawn from the Quality Assurance Unit in Osun State University, Nigeria; the Academic Quality Assurance Unit (AQAU) of the University of Ghana, Ghana, Quality Assurance Unit in the Namibia University of Science and Technology, Namibia and Faculty of Engineering's Quality Assurance Unit, a sub-component of Quality Assurance and Accreditation Centre at Cairo University, Egypt.

For Osun State University, Nigeria, the quality assurance unit is mandated to conduct a host of activities designed to improve the quality of inputs, processes and outputs of the university system. That is, the unit is expected to ensure that the processes and procedures are first and foremost "fit for purpose". Its specific objectives include:

- developing Quality Assurance policy for the university;
- monitoring implementation of the University strategic plan;
- contributing to the achievement of the goals defined for the educational activities and the learning environment;
- monitoring and ensuring that performance processes in all aspects of the University functions are appropriate and relevant;
- appraising flaws and recognizing the strong points of instruction and training;
- serving as a tool for systematic efforts for quality assurance and quality improvement;
- evaluating the quality assurance system periodically;
- coordinating Students' Evaluation of staff and programmes;
- encouraging self-assessment of teaching staff;
- coordinating internal and external assessment of programmes and institution as a whole; and
- organizing capacity building through seminars, workshops and conferences.

The Academic Quality Assurance Unit (AQAU) of the University of Ghana was established in May, 2005 but became operational in August 2007 initially with a staff complement of two, a director at professor level and a principal administrative assistant. The unit's mandate is to contribute to realizing the mission of the University and has the following specific objects:

- advising on academic standards: offer advice to the Academic Curriculum, Quality and Staff Development Committee (ACQSDC) on the determination and maintenance of acceptable levels of academic standards with respect to teaching, learning and research.
- facilitating students' evaluation of courses/lecturers: in collaboration with the Planning & Management Information Services (PMIS) Directorate, conduct student evaluation of courses and teaching staff every semester.

- conducting departmental reviews at least every five years, to be preceded by self-assessment exercises and quality audits.
- facilitating quality audits and staff development: The Unit also facilitates and oversee the preparation of quality audits, self-studies, quality assurance reviews, surveys, staff training and development initiatives
- managing information dissemination on academic quality matters related to quality enhancement to the wider community and beyond.
- Conducting graduate tracer surveys: conducts annual exit surveys of graduating classes and undertake tracer and employer surveys.

Similar services are performed by the Quality Assurance Unit of Namibia University of Science and Technology, Namibia; where the main functions of the unit are to:[65] establish and monitor quality standards and practices; promote a quality culture and quality assurance systems; review and evaluate QA systems and procedures; attend to specific recommendations from faculties; ensure that the various structures of NUST become the drivers of their own quality; and conduct QA related research. Therefore, the key performance areas for the Quality Assurance Unit are:

- Coordination and management of programme accreditation and institutional audits;
- Conducting quality reviews of departments and programmes;
- Managing student evaluations and peer reviews, and
- Management of QA Reports

In Cairo University's Faculty of Engineering a Quality Assurance Unit established in 2003 under the name Self-evaluation and Enhancement Unit, is one of the internal branches of the Quality Assurance and Accreditation Centre at Cairo University. The name change was effected in 2006. The initiative of establishing a centre for evaluation, enhancement and accreditation emerged in 1999 in order to keep up with the requirements of quality assurance and

---

[65]http://www.nust.na/?q=university-administration/quality-assurance/functions-qa-unit

enhancement of education and its rapidly growing importance regionally and globally.[66] The QA unit's vision includes:

- Introduction and establishment of the culture of regular self-evaluation, continuous enhancement and total quality assurance;
- creating a common language for the concept of total quality and developing awareness among the academic community, administration and students at the faculty.
- Ensure quality assurance, accreditation and effective participation in the community services to meet the challenges of the swift progress; and
- win the confidence of the stakeholders in the outputs of the educational system; namely, the graduates, research and professional and community services in conformity with the national, regional and international standards.

To attain the vision, the unit pursues the following strategic objectives:

- Enhancement of the current curricula for undergraduate and graduate programs in all departments of the Faculty;
- Development and implementation of an effective evaluation system for the students, the courses and educational programs, and approving self-evaluation as an input to the internal and external audit and application of quality assurance systems to attain accreditation;
- Introduction and establishment of the culture of regular self-evaluation, continuous enhancement and total quality assurance via creating a common language for the concept of total quality and developing awareness among the academic

---

[66] Faculty of Engineering, Cairo University (n.d.) 'Quality Assurance Unit', http://eng.cu.edu.eg/en/quality-assurance-unit/

- community, administration and students at the faculty to attain quality assurance and accreditation;
- Participation in the community services and meeting the challenges of the swift progress and win the confidence of the stake holders in the outputs of the educational system, namely, the graduates, research and professional and community services in conformity with the national, regional and international standards;
- Design and application of the appropriate model for performance evaluation which integrates all the components of the higher education system and complies with the national, regional and international standards;
- Fully and pragmatically diagnosing the constraints of performance development and proposing solutions and developing enhancement plans;
- Capacity building in the field of performance evaluation and quality assurance and accreditation; and
- Cooperation with the quality assurance and accreditation units and centres, committees, bodies and organizations, at the national and regional levels.

However, the strategic objectives are actualized through a set of activities, some of which are:[67]

- Holding seminars and awareness workshops for quality assurance and the Unit's activities and objectives for Faculty members, teaching assistants, and administration personnel in the Faculty.
- Conducting a wide scope research to identify the systems and mechanisms for quality assurance and accreditation in place world-wide.
- Conducting training courses for staff members in the areas of course and program specification,

---

[67] Faculty of Engineering, Cairo University (n.d.) 'Quality Assurance Unit', http://eng.cu.edu.eg/en/quality-assurance-unit/

- teaching skills and practical training, modern teaching techniques and interactive teaching.
- Organizing workshops for staff members in the areas of self-evaluation strategies, e-learning skills, decision-making, communication skills and time management.
- Preparing a comprehensive program and course specification for all Faculty programs, and Faculty annual reports.
- Preparing regular reports on quality assurance and accreditation in the Faculty.
- Coordination and cooperation with organizations and educational institutions involved in quality assurance and accreditation.
- Organizing field visits to organizations and educational institutions concerned in quality assurance and accreditation.
- Documentation and dissemination of the quality assurance and accreditation systems at the Faculty and establish its sustainability and enhancement.
- Issuing periodic bulletins on the activities and outputs of the Unit.

Quality assurance units in other parts of the world

Two cases consulted for other parts of the world included the Canadian Institute of Technology's Quality Assurance Unit in Canada and Quality Assurance department of the University of Fiji. The unit in Canadian Institute of Technology was first established in the 2012-2013 academic year.[68] Since then the unit has been reorganized several times in order to better reflect the changes of the academic and institutional structures. It is responsible for evaluating and reporting on the quality of education, establishing success measures, implementing best practices and making recommendations for academic improvements. QAU further develops appropriate qualitative and quantitative measures to better assess both academic and other services based on local, regional and

---

[68] CIT Quality Assurance Unit, http://cit.edu.al/en/cit-quality-assurance-unit-cit-qau/

international best practices including standards set by ENQA and other international accreditation boards.[69] Some of QAU competencies:

- Developing policies and procedures with regard to internal quality assurance, which are approved by Academic Senate.
- Assessing periodically the results of teaching and scientific research activities in the main units in accordance with standards.
- Conducting investigative studies to evaluate the efficiency of programs of study and students' employment opportunities.
- At the end of each semester, before the exams, internal quality assurance unit organizes students' survey through questionnaire on the quality of teaching for each subject of study programs.

At the University of Fiji internal quality assurance processes are coordinated by the QA department which was established in 2016. In terms of functions the mandate of the department is to promote and integrate a culture of quality focusing mainly on teaching and learning. The key responsibilities for the unit are to:[70]

- ensure educational improvement and effective performance;
- promote and implement quality-related work in accordance with the university vision and strategic planning;
- ensure efficient monitoring and review of the academic management of courses, teaching and performance;
- support staff development, performance enhancement and opportunities for improvement in teaching;
- monitor staff performance in teaching and learning;

---

[69] http://cit.edu.al/en/cit-quality-assurance-unit-cit-qau/
[70] The University of Fiji (n.d.) 'Quality Assurance Unit', https://www.unifiji.ac.fj/quality-assurance-unit/

- monitor and evaluate student results;
- take into account student feedback to facilitate improved teaching and learning performance;
- develop policies and guidelines on teaching evaluation, programme review and student learning assessment; and
- advise on program and course approval and development.

Reporting structure of quality assurance units

In many institutions that have set up quality assurance units, the unit is headed by a manager or director with reporting line to the head of academic affairs or the head of the institution in some case. The manager or director is expected to have suitable training, and in many cases the qualification required is a doctoral degree, coupled with many years of relevant teaching, research and administrative experience. This is evident from the cases cited below.

- In Palestine Polytechnic University the director reports directly to the president of the university.[71]
- In Osun State University, the Quality Assurance Unit is located in the Vice Chancellor's office though it is headed by a director. There are quality assurance representatives from each faculty and department that work with the Director. The Director is also the chairperson of the implementation/monitoring committee for the strategic plan of the University.[72]
- In University of Patras, Greece there is a unique arrangement without a designated head of quality assurance unit. Instead, the unit comprise:
  - five (5) Faculty members (of the rank of Professor and Associate Professor), one of each School with highly recognized scientific work and, preferably, with experience in quality assurance procedures;

---

[71] Palestine Polytechnic University (https://www.ppu.edu/p/en/administrative-departments/quality-assurance)
[72] http://www.uniosun.edu.ng/index.php/quality-assurance-unit.html

- ➢ four (4) personnel members with the right to vote only when issues concerning them are discussed;
- ➢ a representative of the Special Scientific Personnel;
- ➢ a representative of the Laboratory Teaching Personnel;
- ➢ a representative of the Special Technical and Laboratory Personnel;
- ➢ a representative of the administrative personnel;
- ➢ two (2) representatives of the students with participation rights;
- ➢ a representative of the undergraduate students; and
- ➢ a representative of the postgraduate and PhD students

- In University of Peradeniya the internal quality assurance unit is governed by a management committee, whose membership includes:
  - ➢ a director,
  - ➢ nine (9) faculty coordinators,
  - ➢ a director from staff development centre,
  - ➢ a librarian,
  - ➢ a registrar's nominee,
  - ➢ a bursar's nominee and
  - ➢ a secretary
- The Academic Quality Assurance Unit at University of Ghana is headed by a director. The office has a staff complement comprising an assistant registrar, principal administrative officer, research assistant, a cleaner and four interns serving as part of National Service.[73]
- The Quality Assurance Unit of the Namibia University of Science and Technology is managed by a director who is supported by five QA coordinators and an office administrator.[74]
- Albanian university's Internal Quality Assurance Unit directly reports to the University Senate through the Deputy Rectors of Academic and Research Matters.[75]

---

[73] University of Ghana (n.d.) 'Academic Quality Assurance Unit', http://www.ug.edu.gh/aqau/current-staffs

[74] Namibia University of Science and Technology (n.d.) Quality Assurance Unit, http://www.nust.na/?q=university-administration/quality-assurance/about-qa

[75] Albanian University (n.d.) 'Internal Quality Assurance Unit',

- Universiti Teknologi Brunei the activities of the unit are guided by the Quality Unit Steering Committee.[76]
- The University of Fiji the activities of the unit are coordinated by a team of three quality assurance officers and an academic counsellor.[77]

It appears that just as there is diversity in the name of the units, there is also diversity of administrative arrangements and reporting structures. It is evident that each arrangement is a response to specific operating context. Therefore, it is paramount to note the uniqueness of each institution and endeavour to align the governance of the unit accordingly.

It is also evident that setting up of quality assurance units is a necessary step towards effective and orderly functioning of a modern university. Quality assurance units are not only becoming an integral part of the governance structure of modern universities, but also a key consideration in the business model and operational efficiency of universities. This is a critical trajectory. Such units serve the purpose of linking and coordinating internal and external quality assessments and building synergies in the areas of education, training and research. The effective realization of this expectation requires internal systems and arrangements to entrench a quality culture. A definition of quality culture developed by the European Universities Association in 2006 states that quality culture is:

"organisational culture that intends to enhance quality permanently and is characterised by two distinct elements: a cultural/psychological element of shared values, beliefs, expectations and commitment towards quality and a structural/managerial element with defined processes that enhance quality and aim at coordinating individual efforts." (Matei and Iwinska 2016).[78]

---

http://albanianuniversity.edu.al/en/internal-quality-assurance-unit/
[76] Universiti Teknologi Brunei (n.d.) 'The Quality Assurance Unit', http://www.utb.edu.bn/academics/the-quality-assurance-unit-qau/
[77] The University of Fiji (n.d.) 'Quality Assurance Unit', https://www.unifiji.ac.fj/quality-assurance-unit/
[78] Matei, L. and Iwinska, J. (2016) *Quality Assurance in Higher Education: A Practical Handbook*. Budapest: Central European University and Yehuda Elkana Center for Higher Education.
https://elkanacenter.ceu.edu/sites/elkanacenter.ceu.edu/files/attachment/basicpage/57/qahandbook.pdf

A commitment to promoting a quality culture can be isolated from all the cases mentioned above and more also for Albanian University where it is emphasized that the success of internal quality processes determine to a significant extent the short, medium and long-term performance of the institution and as such requires dedicated and truthful commitment of all its employees, either academic or administrative, current students and alumni.[79] The commitment required for the institutionalization of culture of quality re-affirms the validity of a widely used statement on quality made by William A. Foster who observed that: "Quality is never an accident; it is always the result of high intention, sincere effort, intelligent direction, and skilful execution; it represents the wise choice of many alternatives."[80]

Drawing from the experiences shared above, establishing functional QA units will be a game changer towards quality assurance in public and private higher education institutions in Malawi. This optimism is well founded given that an effective quality assurance unit is a surest way towards institutionalization of a quality culture. It is also one parameter against which institutions can be benchmarked to determine their level of commitment to quality and excellence. Quality units should be able to assure the quality of programmes (curriculum), teaching staff and their teaching, learning resources and experiences, assessment, infrastructure and facilities, among others. Hence, it requires that quality units should be well resourced and empowered to bring together all actors in the quality assurance process. Among these key players are:

- Heads of department who have primary responsibility for the quality and standards in respect of courses and programmes offered by departments;
- Deans of faculty and schools and heads of institutes who are accountable to Senate for the quality of the academic provision within their faculties and schools or institutes;
- Students in each faculty who have a role in ensuring that departments and faculties or schools and institutes deal

---

[79] Albanian University (n.d.) 'Internal Quality Assurance Unit', http://albanianuniversity.edu.al/en/internal-quality-assurance-unit/
[80] The University of Fiji (n.d.) 'Quality Assurance Unit', https://www.unifiji.ac.fj/quality-assurance-unit/

decisively with operational aspects of quality and standards in a manner that enhance their learning experiences;
- University senates which are committed to value of excellence as they have traditionally played the oversight function over quality assurance and enhancement processes by setting procedures for approval, monitoring and review of courses and programmes; approval of assessment results and awards.
- Heads of institution (Vice Chancellors/Rectors) who are expected to provide leadership and oversight with respect to internal quality assurance systems and procedures - development of learning, and quality-related strategy and policy; supporting the faculties and departments in their quality assurance activities and liaising with external stakeholders and professional bodies that also oversee quality and professional development.

For Malawi, Quality Assurance (QA) units are recommended as the surest way of maintaining a desired level of quality which they can exercise through

- Coordination of the development of and updating of Quality Assurance Systems;
- Continuous evaluation of learning, research and community engagement;
- Conducting training workshops to ensure teaching staff are equipped with the requisite skills in quality assurance – pedagogy, curriculum and assessment skills;
- Facilitating self-evaluation processes and following up on all internal and external evaluations
- Carrying out tracer studies to determine the impact of their programmes and in particular perception of quality of the HEIs graduates in the industry;
- Maintaining up-to-date documentation of records and data related to quality assurance processes within the institution; and
- Providing technical support to the development of new courses and programmes.

A critical area is to formalize the establishment and subsequently the institutionalization of quality units through policy, well defined procedures and practices and perhaps enactment of relevant and enabling laws, where it is required. Then, there is a need to ensure appropriate incorporation of the units in the institutional hierarchy and appropriate levels of staffing for effective operationalization of their mandate and functioning. That is, quality assurance units should be structured in a way that they can perform relevant functions, some of which are to promote quality control, accountability, information sharing about quality assurance practices within and outside the institution and support overall institutional improvement. It is necessary that quality requirements are appreciated and pursued from a multidimensional perspective which does not pay lip service to the multiple purposes of enhancing learning and teaching, building trust among stakeholders throughout the higher education systems and increasing awareness and representation of the institution to a spectrum of stakeholders.

In the final analysis, it is proposed that to ensure seamless integration of the quality assurance units the following should be the order.

a) Establishment of Units: There is need for enactment of the legal basis for establishment of quality assurance units in public and private universities. This could be achieved through amendments to the founding mandate of higher education institutions and their governing instruments such as acts, constitutions, statutes and policies. The enactment will eliminate any doubt about the mandate and legality of the units in the management of quality assurance processes.

b) Functions of the QA Unit: The units should have functions that are stated explicitly and that are also clearly demarcated with respect to functions of other units. There should be no duplication of functions while recognizing the complementary functionality of the quality unit with other units or departments. Where other units are performing similar functions, it will be appropriate to review and streamline the performance areas accordingly so that quality units are provided clear and non-conflicting areas of focus for the effective and unhindered development of quality assurance functions and processes.

c) Reporting structure: The establishment of quality assurance units should signify prioritization of quality assurance arrangements, new or revised forms of institutional governance and the professionalization of management of quality assurance. To that extent, the reporting lines should be clearly demarcated and the reporting level should reflect the centrality of the quality assurance function within the structure of each higher education institution.

d) Staffing of QA Unit: The quality assurance unit should have a distinct structure providing professional growth and development for those assigned to support and monitor quality assurance processes. The units should have adequate staff establishments and positions should provide scope for career development in conformity and commensurate with standards in each institution. The terms and conditions should be competitive so that quality assurance units can attract the best, well qualified and experienced staff, who will also deliver the best quality assurance services.

e) QA leadership: The office managing the quality assurance function should enjoy the status befitting a senior scholar and so those appointed to direct and manage its functions must have attained highest academic accolades and preferably those who have progressed in their career to professorial level. The functions must be comprehensive enough to warrant such a placement in the institutional hierarchy.

f) Among other, terms of reference for the office of QA should include the following:

    i) Developing new or reviewing and consolidating existing quality guidelines and regulations for the higher education institution in conformity with the strategic plan;

    ii) Promoting awareness of the provisions for QA;

    iii) Assessing teaching quality and effectiveness through peer group and student review;

iv) Reviewing existing procedures and making changes known to relevant stakeholders;
v) Preparing of tools and procedures for performance evaluation;
vi) Conducting end of programme cycle reviews;
vii) Communicating quality review results and recommendations to all stakeholders;
viii) Analysing past accreditation reports and highlighting areas of remediation in preparation for next evaluation and review exercises;
ix) Monitoring quality, adequacy and currency of facilities and resources;
x) Monitoring compliance in matters such as staff recruitment, staff student ratio, teaching and research quality;
xi) Participating in the review of curricula and evaluation of proposal for new academic programmes;
xii) Organizing regular capacity building and promoting skill acquisition in relevant areas for academic and non-academic staff;

Conclusion

This chapter has drawn from a wide spectrum of experiences from Europe, Asia and Africa about how to set up and operationalize quality assurance units in higher education institutions. It has adequately illustrated the mandates, terms of reference and operational areas envisaged for such units to assure and enhance quality. The case studies cited suggest that higher education institutions around the world have embraced the need to make internal quality visible to the global community of scholars and more especially their clients and users of products of those institutions, including prospective students, parents and guardians, employers, other training institutions and governments, just to mention some. It appears the pursuit of global competitiveness in education and training warrant the practice of displaying quality markers because they have the effect of assuring the global public of the commitment of each institution to quality and excellence. Presence or absence of a functional quality assurance unit, although existence of a QAU is yet to be appropriated for ranking higher education providers globally, is an important indicator of a higher education institution's commitment to quality and competitiveness.

Success of quality assurance units, like most innovations in the field of education, rest on:[81]

a) adequate participation in planning and implementation by all those involved at various levels and stages;
b) support from authorities;
c) sufficient preparation to ensure that those who will be involved and facilities at their disposal will be adequate and capable of meeting the demands placed upon them; and
d) clear identification of the limits within which quality assurance units will operate and the extent of the supporting services that can be harnessed or provided.

While successful operationalization of quality assurance units rest on building upon enabling factors some of which have been listed above, sustainability of units also depend on capacity to mitigate risks and obstacles, for instance, irrelevant curriculum and traditions opposed to curricula innovation; inadequate or lack of financial support and unstable macroeconomic conditions; lack of skilled personnel, inadequate coordination, consultation and therefore lack of consensus; insufficient rewards; and resistance and unsympathetic attitudes by the leadership. The case studies cited above suggest clearly that quality assurance units should focus on strengthening the QA process at institutional level and serve to respond positively to standards and guidelines set by external quality assurance agencies.

---

[81] The four factors were highlighted in an earlier version of a book by J.S. Farrant (1964) titled *Principles and Practice of Education*.

Chapter 8

The Future of Higher Education

Introduction

It is self-evident that access to higher education matters but equally significant is the quality of higher education outcomes- well-trained human resources, critical thinkers and excellent problem solvers. As the demand for higher education is rising exponentially, equally important will be the awareness and commitment to quality by the providers and consumers of higher education so that expanding access does not lead to compromises in quality terms. That is, increasing access and maintenance of desirable quality outcomes are equally important and attainable. Both are in essence governance and management issues. This understanding has been demonstrated throughout the previous chapters and has been the key driver of quality assurance and accreditation in recent times in many developing nations. This chapter will revisit the challenge of expanding access and enhancing quality. Other areas of interest are; the importance of enhancing research capacity and the teaching of sciences- STEM education, enhancing trust in the private provision of higher education and qualifications systems and henceforth mentorship of institutions that will be dedicated to self-learning and community service.

Pragmatic approach to expanding space and access

Student enrolment in Malawi's higher education institutions was 30,972 in 2018, a big jump from 8,168 students enrolled in 2008, while female enrolment in public universities increased from 33% in 2008 to 37.5% in 2018 largely on account of affirmative action (Ministry of Education, 2020). It is evident that the demand for higher education will continue to grow exponentially necessitating expansion of infrastructure in existing higher education institutions or establishment of new institutions altogether in order to meet the rising numbers. It will be safe to state that the demand is likely to rise in proportion to the changes in the population completing secondary education. In terms of space requirements and capacity to support future growth, it is important to reflect on the trajectory witnessed recently. Besides changes in demographics, it is equally important to recognize and pay attention to the policy decisions relating to economic, political or social equality. The response to a question: 'what does the future hold for higher education'; is therefore a complex one. It requires searching for solutions to existing challenges, addressing gaps in the areas of access, quality, market relevance and governance and management as envisaged in the National Education Sector Plan (2008 – 2017) and its successor the National Education Sector Investment Plan (2020 -2030). This is true given that most of the challenges being experienced in the present arise from decisions and policy gaps of the past.

Until the 1990s Malawi had one public university and to date the number of universities has expanded to six, four of which have emerged out of the initial university. The other two have their development trajectories which can be located in the politics of admission to university in the post multiparty political dispensation. These include balancing regional development and expanding space in the wake of resistance to policy on equitable selection or as opponents of the policy put it the re-introduction of quota in university admission. One of the institutions emerged in the 1990s out of a teacher training college that was converted into a university while the other as a new institution, perhaps one of the five (5) universities proposed by the state around 2012 in response to resistance to university quota, what the state had dubbed equitable access. The construction of the new university was made possible by foreign financing won through the diplomatic shift from capitalist to communist China. The construction of what will be the seventh, though it was intended to be the fifth university commenced a couple of years back, but progress has been slow due to financing gaps. It follows that further growth of more public universities is a matter that needs close attention, especially the financing aspect. More public universities can be established by converting and upgrading existing tertiary institutions into universities, unbundling of multi-campus universities or building new institutions, resources permitting. It appears a package combing conversion, upgrading and unbundling of existing institutions is a pragmatic approach to increase the number of institutions, notwithstanding the financial and governance bottlenecks and controversies that such processes tend to generate.

There are abundant lessons to draw from past unbundling. The University of Malawi (previously Chancellor College) started in Blantyre at three premises namely: Chichiri, Soche Hill and Mpemba. Later, Bunda College, The Polytechnic, Kamuzu College of Nursing and College of Medicine became four of the five constituent colleges at its peak. Instead of perceiving unbundling as reversal of a previous process of integration, it is important to perceive it as more of a process of organic growth and maturation. If the emerging institutions can review and expand their programming and eliminate bottlenecks in financing and governance, a healthy competition can be nurtured. Also, as the universities grow and expand by establishing campuses and colleges across the country, the agenda should be to set up and nurture semi-autonomous institutions that will eventually mature into new and autonomous institutes of higher education and universities. It follows that setting up of satellite centres and campuses should be supported by the state and pursued with such a vision. Adequate land, infrastructure development support, staff development initiatives and appropriate administrative arrangements and programming should be envisioned and aligned to the expectation that such centres and campuses will eventually outgrow the parent universities and indeed become autonomous. Infrastructure plans and investments should be aligned to this long term view of organic growth. Nevertheless, it is also pertinent to be open to the idea of integration, where the state can order reorganization of the public higher education landscape in a manner that will facilitate realization of benefits of economies of scale. Geographic considerations can inform a merger of some institutions at some point. The same line of thinking can be postulated for private universities. With the passage of time satellite centres and campuses of private universities should with adequate investment mature into autonomous degree awarding institutions. Hence the number of private institutions is likely to increase and become more diversified requiring such a process that will justify the devolution proposed above. Yet, other institutions may fail to grow or mature and eventually disappear. Among other causative factors may include failure to attract adequate numbers of students such that the operations may become unviable. Other institutions may choose to or forced by circumstances to compromise on quality which may signal their eventual die out. Mergers affecting one or more private higher education institutions are also a possibility. The regulatory regime should be restructured and empowered to guide and respond decisively to such eventualities.

While further growth is expected from a maturing private higher education subsector, the need to define the character of higher education will eventually become a priority. The coming together of institutions of higher learning in the form of voluntary associations will be a step towards that end. These include association of private universities and association of private and public universities and colleges. However, operationalization of the arrangement envisaged above will require a process whereby the leadership will have to define the agenda and philosophy of higher education. Without such a shared vision what will follow will be a disordered growth of institutions or associations whose pursuit for competition and for profit may blur the mission of expanding access to quality higher education. There is a need to reflect on the mission of higher education so that there is consensus especially around capacity, quality and programming issues. For instance, one of the key challenges to date is scarcity of qualified lecturers in many fields. Except for a few institutions, there are significant skill gaps, one indicator being large numbers of first degree holders who have taken up appointments as staff associates/development fellows in public and private institutions, and yet they are required to handle heavy teaching load and sometimes supervise undergraduate research. Institutions struggle to mobilise resources to support their training to masters and later to doctoral level. Given that staff are lacking in terms of postgraduate qualification, the capacity to supervise undergraduate research and offer postgraduate training locally is limited. It will be necessary and important that institutions that have capacity to offer postgraduate training should be supported to channel their energies towards offering of more and diversified high quality postgraduate programmes. A system of institutional support covering infrastructure, equipment, and incentives should be put in place to drive such a cause. More postgraduate programmes will enhance undergraduate programmes especially if the postgraduate students can be engaged as tutors and instructors, releasing the professors and senior lectures to focus on postgraduate supervision, teaching, research, the development of new programmes and projects that add value to postgraduate offerings. Hence, the proposition for older higher education institutions and news ones that have already built up adequate capacity and reputation should be to expand their programming by a focus on higher degrees. Higher degrees will imply enhanced capacity for the sector not just in the areas of teaching and research but also capacity to conduct high impact consultancies and effective and enhanced management of higher education institutions. Postgraduate programmes and training offered locally, if tailor made and responsive to realities on the ground, will certainly advance the national development agenda. Meanwhile, institutions should be cautious of and open to mitigate the risk of intellectual inbreeding.

Balancing access with quality

A study conducted earlier focusing on the University of Malawi observed that the major challenges to quality higher education in Malawi include scarcity and datedness of teaching and learning materials (references books), and under-qualification of academic staff (Msiska and Chulu 2006). To address the problem of quality they proposed a two-pronged approach comprising the raising of tuition fees and deliberate book development and publishing. On fees they proposed raising tuition fees to at least 50% of the economic fee for an undergraduate student per academic year so that money realized from tuition could be used to buy books, laboratory equipment and other teaching and learning materials. On the other hand, they highlighted the need for a deliberate book development and publishing policy by academic staff so that reference materials are readily and locally available. Further, regarding upgrading of staff qualifications they recommended the development and institutionalization of post-graduate programmes while at the same time utilizing staff exchange programmes within Africa, the Southern Africa Development Cooperation (SADC) specifically. Raising tuition has been a heated subject muted in political overtones and contested by student bodies on the premise that raising fees makes higher education inaccessible to the poor. The fees must fall movement has made it even difficult to sustain. As more funding is mobilized to support training institutions, there will be need to ensure adequate support towards gifted students, those from disadvantaged backgrounds whose urgent needs include tuition fees and upkeep and stationery. Existing forms of support are inadequate and in need of reviewing. In view of rising graduate unemployment in the country it is perhaps time to rethink the targeting process to ensure that support is channelled to those pursuing programmes that will allow for the realization of the goals of a revolving fund. There is also a need to address the challenges posed by the lack of credible academic publishers, poor incentives and underdeveloped culture of writing, which have hampered the realization of the vision to promote availability of locally produced books and related materials.

A related contentious issue in higher education has been how to expand the volume of research output, realize high impact publications and enhance global standing of research. This brings into focus the challenges of capacity to conduct research amidst gaps in research funding on one hand and the proliferation of substandard publications and predatory journals on the other. Perhaps more worrying also is the challenge posed by lack of respect for property rights and unethical conduct which appear to impact perceptions of quality. In some cases, the challenge to quality takes the form of plagiarism, a practice which entails unfair use of another person's ideas, information, expressions, or entire work as one's own.[82] It is a violation of academic honesty and integrity given that it impacts on the credibility and trust that the public vests in higher education institutions in general. As the MLA Handbook put it:

> "Plagiarism undermines the relationship between teachers and students, turning teachers into detectives instead of mentors, fostering suspicion instead of trust, and making it difficult for learning to take place. Students who plagiarize deprive themselves of the knowledge they would have gained if they had done their own writing. Plagiarism also can undermine public trust in educational institutions, if students are routinely allowed to pass courses and receive diplomas without doing the required work."[83]

The implications on quality include irreparable breakdown of trust between the upcoming scholar and the seasoned scholar, students and their professors or lecturers and therefore an affront

---

[82] MLA Handbook, 8th Edition. https://style.mla.org/plagiarism-and-academic-dishonesty/
[83] MLA Handbook, 8th Edition. https://style.mla.org/plagiarism-and-academic-dishonesty/

on the hierarchy of learning and scholarly development. Universities around the world have had a fair share of plagiarism. For instance, in Germany plagiarism is a serious concern[84] affecting the credibility of qualifications systems, mainly postgraduate qualifications and the culprits include politically exposed persons (PEPs) or government ministers among regular students (Jimu, 2018). Globally, one of the well-publicised incidence is the withdrawal of a doctoral degree by the University of Düsseldorf in 2013 which was awarded to the then Minister of Education, following allegations and investigations into alleged plagiarism. Two years earlier the Minister of Defence of the same country was forced to resign on account of similar grounds (Altbach 2013). Many government officials and business persons in Russia have also fallen prey to what had been described as "buy a dissertation scandal" (Radyuhin 2013).[85] Some estimates indicate that 30 to 50 per cent of academic degrees awarded in Russia are not earned but purchased and many of the perceived legitimate PhDs have been found to be unworthy due to plagiarism.[86] Outside Europe two academics working for the Dhaka University were accused of co-authorship of an article which included improper citations of materials from Michel Foucault's article titled "The Subject and Power".[87] Plagiarism like fake

---

[84] Based on 2009 figures, out of an estimated 25,000 PhDs awarded every year by German universities, 1000 were reportedly obtained through illicit means. This information is attributed to Manuel René Theisen, professor of business administration at the Ludwig-Maximilians University in Munich, Germany. See Tristana Moore, 'Germany's Ph.D. Scandal: Were Degrees Bought?' *Time*, 28 August 2009.
http://content.time.com/time/world/article/0,8599,1919339,00.html

[85] Statement attributed to Vladimir Filippov, head of the Higher Accreditation Commission in Russia, cited in Vladimir Radyuhin 'Fake doctorates: Russia to crack down on academic fraud', *The Hindu*, 21 February 2013.

[86] It is alleged that PhD dissertations are sold and recently there has been a doubling of price from $5,000 to $10,000. Moscow's prestigious institution, the State Pedagogical University, had its twenty-four out of twenty-five PhD theses checked by a special government commission condemned on account of extensive plagiarism and serious violations of doctoral requirements. In some cases, unscrupulous candidates have copied up to 90 per cent of their dissertations from other sources. See Vladimir Radyuhin 'Fake doctorates: Russia to crack down on academic fraud', The *Hindu*, 21 February 2013.

[87] The accusation related to an article entitled: "A New Dimension of Colonialism and Pop Culture: A case Study of Cultural Imperialism" that was published in Social Science Review. A complaint was lodged by the University of Chicago Press publishers of the article by Foucault. During investigations it emerged that one of the co-authors alleged that the other co-author had inserted

qualifications degrades qualifications and undermines the pursuit of quality education. Fake or counterfeit qualifications debase the pursuit of merit. All employers, both public and private, should close gaps that allow persons to use fake qualifications for employment and promotion. As Blade Nzimande, South Africa's minister of higher education observed on the menace of fake qualifications:

> "Unless employers, institutions and citizens can feel confident that individuals have earned the qualifications that they purport to have, the entire system will lose legitimacy".... "Even the qualifications of those who have obtained them legitimately will be treated with suspicion, and this is unfair to all those who have genuinely worked to acquire such qualifications." .... "Unscrupulous individuals were willing to pay for false qualifications, and have no shame in producing these to support their CVs when applying for jobs, even in our educational institutions."[88]

Therefore, as more universities are introducing or expanding postgraduate programmes, it will be necessity to institute mechanism for detecting such falsehood. Otherwise, fake postgraduate qualification will proliferate and escalate to what it is; a menace to legitimate qualifications. The public should also be made to realize that education cannot be reduced to acquiring or holding of illegitimate qualifications (Jimu 2018). The key pursuit of all higher education institutions should be to provide credible postgraduate training. With a strong and dedicated staff complement, postgraduate students will be taught to the best of the instructors' abilities and resources. Hence, a requirement should be to engage academic staff that have the qualifications and skills that

---

contested material in her portion of the work. While the other claimed that the submission to publishers was made without her consent at a time she was abroad and apparently had filed a complaint to the dean after the articles had been published in her name as the first author. It transpired that the dean's office did not respond to her complaint. Fahim Reza Shovon (2020) "DU finds proof of plagiarism against two teachers", *Dhaka Tribune*.
https://www.dhakatribune.com/bangladesh/education/2020/09/10/du-finds-proof-of-plagiarism-against-two-teachers

[88] 'Fake qualifications undermine education', *News24*,
http://www.news24.com/SouthAfrica/News/Fake-qualifications-undermine-education-20140814

can support students to learn productively, value respect for academic integrity and who will ensure that students are judged and graded fairly and impartially. Respect for conventions of research and scholarship, such as free and open inquiry, appropriate reference to the work of others, and honesty in reporting research findings should be upheld.

Enhancing research and innovation

It follows that besides pursuit for excellence in teaching higher education institutions should also endeavour to enhance their research footprint. Staff should be encouraged and supported to conduct meaningful research, both basic and applied research. The paradox is staff who cannot conduct meaningful research may not be good teachers; especially at postgraduate level where ability to engage in scholarly discourse is critical to effective teaching, and evidence of research is expected as a rule. While public higher education institutions appear to support research and evidence of published research is an established requirement for promotion, in many cases the research agenda is not widely diffused and more often than not some staff do not engage in meaningful scholarly research, and yet, they do not suffer any sense of loss other than that they cannot be promoted. As more private universities are being established there is need for more focus on research which can propel private higher education institutions into the world of knowledge generation and innovation beyond mere dissemination of existing knowledge. Financing research and development (R&D should be given priority. At institutional level, there should be a dedicated budget line for research with an allocation that is sufficient enough to drive the institution's research agenda. Institutional resources should be complemented by a national budget allocation for research and development, for instance, through the National Commission for Science and Technology (NCST). Hence, NCST should be capacitated to operationalize a national research fund that can support research in all fields in both public and private higher education institutions. Such support need not come from the state only, which means that there should be room for private sector involvement in defining and supporting the research agenda and anchoring its funding regime. Injection of private sector resources into the proposed research fund will go a long way to support meaningful research and human capital development on one hand and to the benefit of industry and society on the other. Therefore, besides providing space for internship industry should through dedicated funds towards research shape the research agenda in higher education. Higher education institutions with a significant number of programmes in science, technology, engineering, and mathematics (STEM) require more targeted support to ensure that there is a correct match of programme offerings and the resources required. A point to be emphasized is that university-industry partnerships should encompass knowledge transfer through formal and informal channels, where formal channels would include collaborative research, contract research, academic consultancy, intellectual property (IP) transactions, staff and student mobility providing for periods of hands-on experience in industry. Industry would profit from the highly qualified human resources such as researchers or students on internship, who would in turn have access to technology and expensive research infrastructure. Often, a facet that is neglected is that a successful STEM agenda in higher education requires progressive support to STEM in basic and secondary education, by among other measures, addressing the shortage of qualified STEM teachers in schools, ensuring that curricula is relevant and engaging and resources (laboratories and equipment) are aligned to STEM requirements. A well-qualified cadre of secondary school leavers will address knowledge gaps at the point of admission into university programmes, especially if friendly and inclusive interventions are implemented to uplift learning standards in disadvantaged schools.

As a matter of policy every higher education institution should be able to invest in research in order to contribute to knowledge that can only arise through research focusing on solving known problems, identifying new problems, providing fresh insights, expanding existing knowledge in new ways or creating new artistic works in the arts and humanities. The justification is that no credible higher education institution can thrive on teaching only without a robust research agenda. It also follows that research can be inspired by the desire for discovery through applied research using known methods to specific problems, sometimes in new ways or in new fields, to development or commercialisation, where discoveries are refined for use outside the research environment, to technology transfer, where research findings are used in industry or society. The cardinal point should be to advance the transmission of new knowledge, including sufficient information about the way that knowledge was produced (methods) to enable others to reproduce or validate it and make judgment of its worth through peer review. The implication is that higher education institutions should feel obligated to support the conduct and reporting of research findings ethically and honestly, to establish and consolidate linkages with industry so that more research can be supported by industry and by ensuring that more research is undertaken that leads to direct economic or social advantage or impact on society. Such a process requires better regulation of research through national laws and institutional policies that promote respect for intellectual property, streamlining patenting and commercialization. Such arrangements may promote further research especially if complemented with the establishment of specialized research centres- with niches, centres or institutes established to ensure a 'critical mass' of researchers and enhanced external recognition. The benefits may include improved rating in terms of total research and publications in refereed journals, number of competitive research grants awarded on the basis of the researcher's proposal and track record; numbers and quality of the doctoral theses; and the number of patents. This is necessary if higher education institutions are to maintain credibility and shed off the status of being "glorified high schools" (Msiska 2008). According to Msiska glorified high schools are "unable to produce the kind of graduate required for engendering, monitoring and reviewing development processes in a country and unable to conduct research to inform attendant challenges" (Msiska 2008:7).

Cultivating trust in higher institutions

Rising graduate unemployment makes this observation a key area for consideration. The challenge of underemployment is a real one in some sectors and the loss of value of qualifications as jobs requiring low level skills, training and qualifications become attractive to those with higher qualifications. That is, the inflation of qualifications raises a quality and governance issue that higher education institutions, both public and private, should contribute to addressing.

Older institutions have a role to nurture new and budding institutions. This requires some form of mentorship through partnerships involving pairing of new and older institutions, where the older institutions can guide and mentor the new institutions. The scope and terms of mentorship would vary between institutions from the terms negotiated between the new and older institutions concerned. However, it will be important that the mentorship should include matters of curriculum and programme development, pedagogy, measurement, testing and evaluation and above all benchmarking to best practices. One of the key areas for benchmarking should be institutionalization and operationalization of quality assurance processes – admission of students, recruitment and training of staff, pedagogy and assessment, just to mention some.

Older higher education institutions should be open and responsive to global trends, for instance, aligning their internal quality processes to the new norm involving external quality control and regulation. It is important also to align national practices to relevant regional, continental and international trends. Participation in regional and international networks, and supporting harmonization of quality assurance processes should be given priority. It is necessary that higher education institutions should become active participants in the associations such as Association of African Universities (AAU), Southern Africa Regional Universities Association (SARUA) and others. Quality assurance agencies and units should also become actively linked to bodies such as Southern Africa Quality Assurance Network (SAQAN), Harmonization of African Higher Education, Quality assurance and Accreditation (HAQAA), International Network of Quality Assurance Agencies in Higher Education (INQAAHE), among others. Another topical area is finalization of the development of a national qualifications framework (NQF), which should be informed by practices in the region, in Africa and global trends and practices. An important observation is that NQFs can serve as a useful tool in education and training reforms, providing key reference points for monitoring whether students are learning relevant skills that respond to socioeconomic and labour market needs. Effective coordination of NQFs at regional and sub-regional levels is worth advocating for as it can facilitate labour mobility and increase job prospects for graduates from the higher education institutions. It is also important to determine appropriate and adequate levels of support towards realizing the goal of promoting the learning outcomes perspective; making higher education qualifications systems easier to understand both nationally and internationally; strengthening the coherence of qualifications systems and connecting different parts of education and training and making it easier to understand and articulate; improve permeability of education and training by clarifying and strengthening the horizontal and vertical links; supporting lifelong learning; strengthening the link and improving the communication between education and training on one hand and the labour market on the other; and providing clear reference points for quality assurance (Raffe 2009).

There is a need to tame the proliferation of unwarranted honorary doctorates and buy a degree schemes perpetrated by some institutions, local and foreign institutions as well. It is conventional practice that honorary degrees are awarded in honour or for the sake of honour (*honoris causa*) or to the honour (*ad honorem*) of a person in respect of their contribution to society.[89] The use of the title "Dr. (hc)"; the letters hc standing for honoris causa; signify that the award was not earned per standard academic practice. To that extent, awardees and the public should desist from confusing such awards with 'real' degrees. Honorary degrees are shadow qualifications. Perhaps it is necessary to underscore that granting or receiving a doctorate or any other qualification as an honour does not result in instant education in favour of the recipient. As Kenneth Dipholo (2014) observed, honorary degrees are just stupefying and misleading decorations that give recipients a false sense of importance.[90] Therefore, higher education institutions

---

[89] Bhanver, J. (2018) 'Honorary Doctorates for sale', https://www.linkedin.com/pulse/honorary-doctorates-sale-jagmohan-bhanver

[90] Dipholo observed that the proliferation of honorary doctorates as opposed to those earned gives a bad reputation in the following words: "Thus, the award of honorary doctorates has become such an unregulated business where seemingly any bogus institution that pretends to be of higher learning could simply pick a clown or sleepwalker to confer an honorary degree. It would not be surprising in the future when it is discovered that the majority of those using the title never actually attended high school and literally outnumber those who earned the degree. For those who have worked so hard to qualify for the degree, it is sickening to be bandied together with school loafers and put in the same league with such proud perverts and excessively conceited despots that have been decorated with the title. In fact, it is so nauseating to be addressed as 'Dr' so and so hence many substantive holders of the title prefer the simple all-round title of

should pay close attention to what they do. They should avoid trivialization that may arise from honorary titles bestowed to members of the public for political convenience. In the past Councils of Mzuzu University and University of Malawi awarded honorary doctorate degrees to spouses of former presidents and such awards were generally considered politically motivated.

Where merit is the rule there can be no plausible justification for watering down criteria in order to accommodate less qualified candidates. Setting standards so low that certain categories of staff would rise to senior positions or get promoted to senior lecturer or professor level defeat the purpose, which is pursuit for quality and excellence. It is perhaps one of the worst forms of compromises on integrity in higher education. Such tendencies and practices, which are more likely to happen in institutions lacking traditions of academic excellence, are also bound to happen in public universities where staff have been pushing for the watering down of promotion criteria which they consider to be too restrictive to their upward movement and in a few circumstances some have challenged well-meaning reviews and application of revised promotion criteria that prohibit presentation and consideration of articles published in predatory journals. Writing on the subject of 'corrupt schools and colleges', Hallak and Poisson (2007) noted that the higher education sector world over faces significant difficulties ranging from financial constraints; weak management; low efficiency; wastage of resources; low quality of service delivery; lack of relevance as illustrated by high unemployment of graduates. The award of politically transmitted doctoral titles (including the honorary titles) and the push for accelerated promotions are facets of academic corruption that higher education institutions should guard against. Higher education institutions should be ready to unlearn and forgo practices that accommodate gross comprises in quality, should be open to learning from others and endeavour to adopt best practices that would facilitate growth and improvement in their programme offerings, administrative and financial management capacities and standing in the global community of higher education institutions. Benchmarking of processes and practices is therefore strongly

---

'Mr' that hardly gives people any special place in society." Dipholo, K. (2014) 'Linkokwing Honorary Doctorates are an Insult to Tertiary Education', http://www.sundaystandard.info/linkokwing-honorary-doctorates-are-insult-tertiary-education

advocated. Programmes, recruitment of staff, admission and assessment of students should be managed in a manner that would lead to attainment of quality and excellence. It calls for openness to opportunities, willingness to learn from others and let others critique what works and how systems, processes and procedures may be improved upon. Hence, there is a need for a break to insularity, mediocrity and complacency.

Self-learning, continuous improvement and community orientation of institutions

There is a need to inculcate a culture of self-assessment conducted on regular basis to inform continuous improvement. Such reviews should be complemented by externally sanctioned quality reviews and audits. The benefits include informed and more objective evaluations; better awareness of the performance and effectiveness of quality assurance and quality control systems and procedures; enhanced accountability of departments, faculties and management; readiness in terms of meeting expectations and requirements of external quality assurance bodies; improved institutional ability to prioritise issues and effective decision-making, and opportunities for disseminating good practices; raising awareness of quality issues within the institution and team-building where there is good level of staff involvement and participation. Yet, higher education institution need to mitigate the associated challenges which include costs, constraints of sustaining commitment among review teams and managing expectations, discouragement and fatigue that may arise, especially in the initial rounds of self-assessment.

Inclusive and good quality higher education is necessary for the formation of a dynamic, well-informed and equitable society. Therefore, higher education institutions should review and enhance their level of commitment to society through community service and engagement. Beyond serving society and educating the nation, which is their core business, higher education institutions may benefit society more if they can be progressive in the area of outreach, especially focusing on immediate communities. Professors regardless of their field of specialisation can be of greater service to the teaching profession if they can take on roles of facilitating civic engagement, advancing the teaching and learning in their areas of specialisation, drawing up guidelines for ethical and professional conduct, being mentors, serving as a reviewers, among others. They can also be of service to the wider community by educating the masses through the medium of public lectures or providing objective and balanced commentary on public issues of the day. It is notable that some members of the academy, for instance, the law faculty provide legal assistance to disadvantaged groups and those in nursing and medicine combine academic and professional (clinical) practice, while others provide extension services and pastoral care and guidance thereby enhancing the welfare of the public through such endeavours. It is also possible for colleges and universities to reach out to the community at large by providing open but regulated access to their facilities including libraries, sporting facilities, meeting rooms, etc. Also, higher education institutions (especially public ones) should be open to the possibility of opening up their programmes or part thereof to the wider audience through open learning offered free of charge to those who would want to learn on their own, with no assessment involved or credits awarded by harnessing and widening access to their open and online learning platforms. A related area is the need to establish new and strengthen existing ties, alliances and collaborations with other higher education institutions nationally, regionally and internationally. These initiatives should be complemented by robust public relations and marketing platforms. Effective communication is advocated not merely as a means to market programmes, innovations and partnerships but also as a measure of the commitment of the institutions to community outreach, as part of the collaboration with industry, willingness to share information, commitment to integrity, transparency and accountability. Perhaps, the limiting factor is reticence in sharing information or data. Institutions are unwilling to disclose information including that on enrolment such that it is hardly possible for outside stakeholders and authorities in the Ministry of Education to know enrolment per programme, staff profiles and even compliance levels with respect to statutory requirements.[91]

In the final analysis a well governed higher education sector is a necessary condition for the realization of equitable and market

---

[91] The Education Management Information Systems (EMIS) report for 2021, *Malawi Education Statistics Report*, produced by the Ministry of Education shows clearly that most private universities did not submit the required data.

relevant higher education. It is incumbent upon all stakeholders to play their rightful roles to make it possible. Yet, it is also true that higher education institutions retain the primary responsibility whether it is dictated by law or provided in a policy or learned through intuition or a willingness to adopt and conform to conventional and sector specific best practices. This proposition applies equally to proprietors, shareholders, managers and students pursuing higher education. The complementarity of systematic external quality control (including institutional registration, audits and accreditations or ranking systems) and internal mechanisms for monitoring and enhancing quality or compliance with respect to internal benchmarks cannot be stressed.

References

African Union Commission (2018) African Quality Rating Mechanism (AQRM) Consolidated Evaluation Report.

Albanian University (n.d.) 'Internal Quality Assurance Unit', http://albanianuniversity.edu.al/en/internal-quality-assurance-unit/

Assié-Lumumba, N.T. (2006) *Higher Education in Africa: Crises, reforms and transformations.* Dakar; CODESRIA Working Chapter series.

Assié-Lumumba, N.T. (2006). *Higher Education in Africa: Crises, reforms and transformations.* Dakar: CODESRIA Working Chapter Series.

Ayewole, O. (2010) "The African Quality Rating Mechanisms: The Process, Prospects and Risks". (Key-Note Address), Fourth International Conference on Quality Assurance in Higher Education in Africa and Capacity Building (Training) Workshop (ICQAHEA-2010) Bamako, October 5-7 (Conference); 8-9 (Workshop), 2010. http://ifgu.auf.org/media/document/KEYNOTE_Oye_AQRM_Process-Prospect_and_Risks_2.pdf

Banerjee, A. Hanna, R. and Mullainathan, S. (2009) 'Corruption' http://econ-www.mit.edu/files/3848

Biogioli, M. (2002) 'From book censorship to academic peer review.' *Emergences*, vol. 12, No. 1, pp. 11 -45. https://doi.org/10.1080/1045722022000003435

Blessinger P. et al (2018), Towards a more equal, inclusive higher education, University World News, The Global Window on Higher Education, ttps://www.universityworldnews.com/post.php?story=20180306102731111.

Cadena, S., García, G.L, Loza-Aguirre, E.F., Ortiz, J., Pérez, A. and Segura-Morales, M.A. (2018) "Measuring Quality of Higher Education", 10th International Conference on Education and New Learning Technologies. DOI:10.21125/edulearn.2018.2484

Čerešňová .Z (2018), INCLUSIVE HIGHER EDUCATION, Nakladatelství Gasset – Allan Gintel, Czech Republic, Prague, 2018

Chan, R. Y. (2016). 'Understanding the purpose of higher education: An analysis of the economic and social benefits for completing a college degree. *Journal of Education Policy, Planning and Administration, 6(5)*, 1-40. Retrieved from: http://www.jeppa.org. (Accessed on 11th July 2018).

Chapleo, C. and Simms, C. (2010) *Stakeholder analysis in higher education: A case study of the University of Portsmouth*. CIT Quality Assurance Unit, http://cit.edu.al/en/cit-quality-assurance-unit-cit-qau/

Clarke, M. (2002) 'Some Guidelines for Academic Quality Rankings', *Higher Education in Europe*, Vol. XXVII, No. 4, 2002. http://siteresources.worldbank.org/INTAFRREGTOPTEIA/Resources/acad_qual_rank_guide.pdf

Council for Higher Education (CHE) *Minimum Programme Accreditation Standards for Higher Education Institutions in Lesotho*. http://www.che.ac.ls/documents/Accreditation_Standards.pdf

Dewey, J. (1934). "Individual Psychology and Education," *The Philosopher*, 12, 1934.

Dillon, A. (n.d.) 'Education in Plato's Republic' https://www.scu.edu/character/resources/education-in-platos-republic/ (accessed on 10th July, 2018)

Dipholo, K. (2014) 'Linkokwing Honorary Doctorates are an Insult to Tertiary Education', http://www.sundaystandard.info/linkokwing-honorary-doctorates-are-insult-tertiary-education

Durkheim's Perspective on Education https://revisesociology.com/2017/08/22/functionalist-durkheim-role-education/

Elmuti, D. and Kathawala, Y. (1997) 'An overview of benchmarking process: a tool for continuous improvement and competitive advantage', *Benchmarking for Quality Management and Technology*, 4 (4), pp. 229-243

Faculty of Engineering, Cairo University (n.d.) 'Quality Assurance Unit', http://eng.cu.edu.eg/en/quality-assurance-unit/

Farrant, J.S. (1964) *Principles and Practice of Education*. Longman

Freire, P. (1992). 'The Purpose of Education", Extract from "The 40th Anniversary of the UNESCO Institute for Education", UIE Reports No. 6, 1992. http://www.unesco.org/education/pdf/FREIRE.PDF

Studies in Ethnomethodology

Garwe, E.C. (2015). 'Qualification, Award and Recognition Fraud in Higher Education in Zimbabwe'. *Journal of Studies in Education* 5(2): 119–135.

González, M.C. (2003) 'An ethics for postcolonial ethnography', in R.P Clair (ed.) *Expressions of Ethnography: novel approaches to qualitative methods*, pp. 77 – 86. Albany: State University of New York.

Grant Harman (1996) Quality Assurance for Higher Education: Developing and Managing Quality Assurance for Higher Education Systems and Institutions in Asia and The Pacific, Asia-Pacific Centre of Educational Innovation for Development (ACEID) Bangkok.
http://unesdoc.unesco.org/images/0010/001040/104046E.pdf

Hall. N and Mambo. M (2015) Education for Development (2015), Financing Education in Malawi Opportunities for Action, Country Case Study for the Oslo Summit on Education for Development, 6 -7 July, 2015.

Hallak, J. and Poisson, M. (2007) *Corrupt schools, corrupt universities: What can be done?* UNESCO: International Institute for Educational Planning.

Harman, G. (1996) 'Quality Assurance for Higher Education: Developing and Managing Quality Assurance for Higher Education Systems and Institutions in Asia and The Pacific', Asia-Pacific Centre of Educational Innovation for Development (ACEID) Bangkok.
http://unesdoc.unesco.org/images/0010/001040/104046E.pdf

Heller, N. (2008) 'Defining and measuring corruption: where have we come from, where are we, and what matters for the future?', XIII Congreso Internacional del CLAD sobre la Reforma del Estado y de la Administración Pública, Buenos Aires, Argentina, 4 - 7 November, 2008.

International Institute for Educational Planning
http://unesdoc.unesco.org/images/0026/002613/261356e.pdf

Jegede, A. (2012) 'The Status of Higher Education in Africa', Being an invited contribution to the Panel Discussion in the Launch of *Weaving Success: Voices of Change in African Higher Education*- A project of the Partnership for Higher Education in Africa (PHEA) held at the Institute of International Education, 809 United Nations Plaza, New York, NY 10017, on Wednesday, February 1, 2012.
https://www.carnegie.org/media/filer_public/5e/d0/5ed04cc9-b250-48e5-b9ee-dd97b3f9139a/ccny_speech_2012_status.pdf

Jimu, I.M. (2016) *Moving in Circles: Underdevelopment and uncertainty in the global periphery.* Langaa Research & Publishing CIG.

Jimu, I.M. (2018) 'Fake qualifications and the challenge of regulating higher education in Southern Africa', *Modern Africa: Politics, History and Society*, 6(1), pp. 107 – 134.

Jimu, I. and Sadalaki, J. (2021) 'Promotion of Inclusive Tertiary Education in the Context of the World Bank Financed Skills Development Project in Malawi' A paper presented at the Higher Education International Conference, Sunbird Nkopola Lodge, Mangochi, Malawi from 24th to 25th June 2021.

Jongbloed, B (2007) 'On Governance, Accountability and the Evaluative State', *Towards a Cartography of Higher Education Policy Change*, pp. 133 – 138.

Kadzamira, E. and Rose, P., 2001, 'Educational Policy Choice and Policy Practice in Malawi: Dilemmas and Disjunctures', IDS Working Paper no. 124, Institute of Development Studies, Brighton.

Kaufmann D. and Kraay, A. (2003) 'Governance Indicators: Where Are We, Where Should We Be Going?' The World Bank, Policy Research Working Chapter 4370

Kaufmann, D. Kraay, A. and Mastruzzi, M. (2005) 'Measuring Governance Using Cross-Country Perceptions Data', The World Bank.

Kaufmann, D., Kraay, A. and Zoido - Lobatón, P. (2000) 'Governance Matters: From Measurement to Action ' *Finance & Development*, June 2000.

Kehinde, A.L. (n.d.) 'Quality Assurance Unit', http://www.uniosun.edu.ng/index.php/quality-assurance-unit.html

Kennison, R. (2016) "Back to the Future: (re)turning from Peer Review to Peer Engagement," *Learned Publishing* 29, no. 1 (January 1, 2016): 69, doi:10.1002/leap.1001.

Kis, V. (2005) 'Quality Assurance in Tertiary Education: Current Practices in OECD Countries and a Literature Review on Potential Effects', Institut d'Etudes Politiques de Paris (Sciences Po), France. https://www.oecd.org/education/skills-beyond-school/38006910.pdf

Lester, S. (1999) 'An introduction to phenomenological research', https://www.rgs.org/CMSPages/GetFile.aspx?nodeguid=7ad9b

8d4-6a93-4269-94d2-585983364b51&lang=en-GB (accessed on 4th January, 2022)

Magalhaes, A. and Veiga, A. (2018) The Evaluative State, Higher Education, Encyclopedia of International Higher Education Systems and Institutions

Marshall S.J. (2018) 'Internal and External Stakeholders in Higher Education', *Shaping the University of the Future*. Springer, Singapore. Pp. 77-102.

Martin, M. (2000) *Managing university-industry relations: a study of institutional practices from 12 different countries*. Working document in the series: Improving the managerial effectiveness of higher education institutions. International Paris: Institution for Education Planning, UNESCO.

Masanja, V. G. and Lwakabamba, S. (n.d) 'Liberalization of higher education in Sub-Saharan Africa', RUFORUM Working Document Series (ISSN 1607-9345) No. 14 (2): 1-7 Available from *http://repository.ruforum.org*

Matei, L. and Iwinska, J. (2016) *Quality Assurance in Higher Education: A Practical Handbook*. Budapest: Central European University and Yehuda Elkana Center for Higher Education. https://elkanacenter.ceu.edu/sites/elkanacenter.ceu.edu/files/attachment/basicpage/57/qahandbook.pdf

Materu, P. (2007) *Higher Education Quality Assurance in Sub-Saharan Africa: Status, Challenges, Opportunities, and Promising Practices*. Washington, D.C.: The International Bank for Reconstruction and Development/The World Bank.

Ministry of Education, Science and Technology (2008). *National Education Sector Plan 2008 – 2017*. Lilongwe: Government of Malawi.

Ministry of Education (2020) *National Education Sector Investment Plan 2020 – 2030*. Lilongwe: Ministry of Education.

Msiska, F.GW (2008) "The Brain Drain-Gain, Quality of Higher Education and Development in Malawi" http://www.nuigalway.ie/dern/documents/65_fred_gennings_wanyavinkhumbo_msiska.pdf

Msiska, F.GW and Chulu, B. (2006) 'Curriculum Reform and Quality Higher Education in the University of Malawi: A Study of the Current State of Affairs', Paper Presented at Regional Eastern Africa UNISTAFF Alumni Network 1st International Conference and Workshop on "Quality Assurance in Higher

Education": 6 – 10 November 2006, Kenyatta University, Nairobi, Kenya.

Mishra, S (2006) *Quality Assurance in Higher Education: An Introduction.* Bangalore: National Assessment and Accreditation Council (NAAC). http://naac.gov.in/images/docs/Resources/Toolkit4Tr_Edctn_Institution/QAHE-Book.pdf

Namibia University of Science and Technology (n.d.) Quality Assurance Unit, http://www.nust.na/?q=university-administration/quality-assurance/about-qa

National Council for Higher Education (2015) *Minimum Standards for Higher Education Institutions.* Lilongwe.

Ncube, A and Tshabalala .T (2014) Barriers to the Implementation of Inclusive Education in Teachers' Colleges in Zimbabwe, *Journal of Humanities and Social Sciences,* Vol. 3 (3).

Ndhlovu, E. (n.d.) 'Malawi working hard to improve education for social development' https://www.mbc.mw/index.php/news/sports/item/5858-malawi-working-hard-to-improve-education-for-social-development

Nyamnjoh, F. (2012) 'Potted Plants in Greenhouses': A Critical Reflection on the Resilience of Colonial Education in Africa', *Journal of Asian and African Studies,* 47(2) 129–154

Nyangau, J. Z. (2014). 'Higher Education as an Instrument of Economic Growth in Kenya'. *FIRE: Forum for International Research in Education* 1(1). Available at: http://preserve.lehigh.edu/fire/vol1/iss1/3 (25 January 2017).

Oduaran, A. and Oduaran, C. 'Widening Access to University Education in Anglophone Africa: Problems and prospects' paper presented at The Community University of the Valleys Partnership International Conference on 'Changing Landscapes' held at the University of Wales, Swansea, U.K. 11th & 12th April, 2005

Palestine Polytechnic University (https://www.ppu.edu/p/en/administrative-departments/quality-assurance)

Parankimalil, J. (2012) "Meaning, nature and aims of education", https://johnparankimalil.wordpress.com/2012/03/26/meaning-nature-and-aims-of-education/

Pontille, D. and Torny, D. (2014) "The Blind Shall See! The Question of Anonymity in Journal Peer Review," *Ada: A Journal of Gender, New Media, and Technology*, April 21, 2014.

Prasad, V S and Stella, A. (n.d.) "Best Practices Benchmarking in Higher Education for Quality Enhancement", *Best Practices in Higher Education*. http://naac.gov.in/docs/Best%20Practices/Best%20Practise%20in%20Higher%20Education.pdf

Radyuhin, V. 'Fake doctorates: Russia to crack down on academic fraud', *The Hindu*, 21 February 2013

Raffe. D. (2009). *National Qualifications Frameworks in Ireland and Scotland: A Comparative Analysis*. Available from Internet: http://www.ces.ed.ac.uk/PDF%20Files/NQF_ECER_2009.pdf [cited 25.05.2010].

Republic of Malawi (2011) *National Council for Higher Education Act*.

Republic of Namibia, *Criteria for Accreditation of New Programmes*. http://www.unam.edu.na/wp-content/uploads/2014/06/NCHE-QualityAssuranceSystemforHigherEducationinNamibia_000.pdf

Ryan, T. (2015) 'Quality Assurance in Higher Education: Review of Literature', *Higher Learning Resources* Communication, 5(4). https://files.eric.ed.gov/fulltext/EJ1132941.pdf

Salmi, J. (2009) *The Challenge of Establishing World-Class Universities*. Washington DC: The International Bank for Reconstruction and Development / The World Bank

Savga, L., Krykliy, O. and Kyrychenko, K. (2018) 'The Role of Internal and External Stakeholders in Higher Education System in Ukraine', *Business Ethics and Leadership*. Vol. 2, No. 1. Pp 32 – 43. (https://www.researchgate.net/publication/324566083_The_Role_of_Internal_and_External_Stakeholders_in_Higher_Education_System_in_Ukraine)

Southern Association of Colleges and Schools, Commission on Colleges 'Guidelines for Addressing Distance and Correspondence Education'. http://www.sacscoc.org/pdf/081705/Guidelines%20for%20Addressing%20Distance%20and%20Correspondence%20Education.pdf

Srivasatava, S. (2015) "Fake degrees is not the problem, obsession with degrees is" *The Wire*, 15/07/2015. Available online:

https://thewire.in/education/fake-degrees-is-not-the-problem-obsession-with-degrees-is (last accessed on 11 February, 2022)

Tanzania Commission for Universities (2012) Tanzania University Level Education: Minimum Guidelines and Norms for Governance Units. http://www.tcu.go.tz/images/pdf/Minimum%20Guidelines%20Norms%20%20for%20Governance%20Units.pdf

The Africa-America Institute (2015) State of Education in Africa Report 2015; A report card on the progress, opportunities and challenges confronting the African education sector. https://www.aaionline.org/wp-content/uploads/2015/09/AAI-SOE-report-2015-final.pdf

The University of Fiji (n.d.) 'Quality Assurance Unit', https://www.unifiji.ac.fj/quality-assurance-unit/

The World Bank (2010). *The Education System in Malawi*, World Bank Working Chapter No 182.

The World Bank (1994) Higher Education: The lessons of experience. Washington DC: IBDR/The World Bank

Thiaw, I. (2007). 'Challenges facing the university in Africa'. *Social Dynamics* 33(1): 232–237.

United Nations (n.d.) Transforming Our World: The 2030 Agenda for Sustainable Development (A/RES/70/1). https://sustainabledevelopment.un.org/content/documents/21252030%20Agenda%20for%20Sustainable%20Development%20web.pdf

Universiti Teknologi Brunei (n.d.) 'The Quality Assurance Unit', http://www.utb.edu.bn/academics/the-quality-assurance-unit-qau/

University of Ghana (n.d.) 'Academic Quality Assurance Unit', http://www.ug.edu.gh/aqau/about-academic-quality-assurance-unit

University of Kent (n.d.) 'Unit of the Enhancement of Learning & Teaching', https://www.kent.ac.uk/uelt/about/quality.html

University of Lisboa (n.d.) 'The Quality Assurance and Assessment Office', https://www.ulisboa.pt/en/info/quality-assurance-and-assessment-office-0

University of Malawi (2012) *UNIMA Strategic Plan 2012 – 2017*. Zomba.

University of Patras (n.d) https://www.upatras.gr/en/modip

University of Peradeniya (n.d.) Internal Quality Assurance Unit', https://www.pdn.ac.lk/centers/iqau/intdu.php

University of Vienna (n.d.) 'Quality Assurance', http://www.qs.univie.ac.at/en/

Usher, A. and J. Medow (2010). *Global Higher Education Rankings 2010, Affordability and accessibility in comparative perspective.* Toronto: Higher Education Strategy Associates.

Uva Wellassa University (n.d.) 'Internal Quality Assurance Unit' (IQAU) http://www.uwu.ac.lk/academic/units/iqau/ .

Van Leeuwen, T. (2007) 'Legitimation in discourse and communication', https://doi.org/10.1177%2F1750481307071986

Vannini, P. (ed.) (2009) 'Introduction', *Material Culture and Technology in Everyday Life: Ethnographic approaches*, pp. 1 – 12. New York: Peter Lang.

Von Haldenwang, C. (2017) 'The Relevance of Legitimation – A New Framework for Analysis', *Contemporary Politics* 23(3):269-286

Wicks, S. (1992) 'Peer review and quality control in higher education', *British Journal of Higher Educational Studies*, Vol. XXXX No. 1

Wilger, A (1997) 'Quality Assurance in Higher Education: A Literature Review', Stanford University: National Center for Postsecondary Improvement. https://web.stanford.edu/group/ncpi/documents/pdfs/6-03b_qualityassurance.pdf

Zimerman, M. (2012) "Plagiarism and international students in academic libraries", New Library World, Vol. 113 No. 5/6, pp. 290-299. https://doi.org/10.1108/03074801211226373

www.ingramcontent.com/pod-product-compliance
Lightning Source LLC
Chambersburg PA
CBHW021711230426
43668CB00008B/803